AND CATCH THE HEART OFF GUARD

Brian D'Arcy

And Catch the Heart Off Guard

the columba press

First published in 2015 by
the columba press
55A Spruce Avenue, Stillorgan Industrial Park,
Blackrock, Co. Dublin

Cover design by Helene Pertl I Columba Press
Origination by The Columba Press
Printed by ScandBook

The title is taken from 'Postscript' by Seamus Heaney,
The Spirit Level (Faber & Faber, London, 2001)

ISBN 978 1 78218 256 6

PREFACE

I'll admit it now! This is the book I didn't want to write. It is the book the publishers encouraged me to compile for more than ten years now and which I steadfastly resisted.

Why? It's a long story.

When I prepare my Sunday sermons, I spend an inordinate amount of time reading, studying, praying and then reflecting on what I should say to our faithful congregation at multiple Masses each weekend. I have been following the same laborious routine at St Gabriel's Retreat, the Graan for twenty years or so.

I never write sermons before I preach, but each Sunday night I put the salient points of the homily on paper to be typed up later in the week. I save them, and when the relevant Sunday, in the three-year cycle, comes around again, I check what I said three years ago. I'll repeat a story or an insight but, mostly, I make sure not to preach the same sermon year after year.

I find preaching the Sunday homily challenging. Yet I recognise that most people at our Masses relish the challenge. They long to be comforted by God's Word. They need, and appreciate, an inspiring, practical thought to get them through the week. They want to live their faith and to believe their religion is still relevant.

The publishers tried to persuade me that jottings from these sermons would do precisely that. A book of spiritual thoughts would be valuable not only for those who attend our Masses, but even more so for those who can't come to the Graan every week.

I still wasn't convinced. Sermons are relevant on the particular Sunday they are preached and that's the main reason I didn't want them in a book.

Now add in countless sermons for Novenas, special occasions, weddings, funerals, bereavement nights and prayer groups. You can readily see why searching through close on half a million words would be futile.

But, they argued, the central theme of a homily remains relevant because gospel truths continue to guide and inspire.

Earlier this year by way of twisting my arm, it was suggested to me that Angela Hanley, a theologian, lecturer and writer was willing to sift through some material and that she, not me, would decide if there was anything worth gathering for a book.

I am forever grateful to Angela for taking on the task. She has done a magnificent job and has found passages, thoughts and opinions which I hope will be useful to any interested person in search of spiritual encouragement in our busy world. So if you find anything useful in this book then the thanks is entirely due to Angela. Her insightfulness, hard work and ongoing gentle direction, have added something special to this collection. I am humbled that a person of Angela's standing could find anything worthwhile in what I preached.

For the most part her selections are short and to the point. They are meant to spark a thought of comfort, peace or perhaps prayer within the reader. I think it's best to pick and choose your own way through the book as the Holy Spirit suggests, rather than read it from cover to cover.

Little of what I preached is original. I have prayed my way through a wealth of homiletic material. For that reason I am grateful to the many authors I've read. Their writings inspired me and hopefully what I found useful will inspire you.

In our oratory each night I end the day with prayer before the Blessed Sacrament. On many occasions I come into God's presence completely empty-handed. I have a Bible and one or two other books similar to this one which I invariably glance at. The Holy Spirit never fails to find something comforting for me to end my day with. I suggest that could be the best way for you to use this book too.

As well as thanking Angela Hanley and all at Columba Press involved in its production, I need to acknowledge the generations of people in the pews who listened carefully and were wise enough to pass on to me what they found useful and relevant – and what they didn't!

The readers of the *Sunday World* will recognise some of the thoughts here, as indeed will the listeners to *Pause for Thought* on BBC Radio 2 with Chris Evans, and *Sunday with Brian D'Arcy* on BBC Radio Ulster. Thanks for your emails, tweets and texts. But all of these thoughts have been shared initially with our Sunday congregation at some time.

In particular I thank our community and staff at the Graan without whose support I would have floundered in recent years.

Finally I would like you to know that any profits from this book, and I realise they will not be great, will go directly to the poor and needy. As always, the money will be donated to agencies caring for refugees across Europe. It will be a minor contribution to a major problem.

May God reward all those generous people who have influenced my journey in life and may this book provide you with a few signposts on your journey now.

Brian D'Arcy,
October 2015

INTRODUCTION

Two weeks before he died, I went to see Seamus Heaney read poetry in the Millennium Theatre, Derry. The piper Liam O'Flynn was also performing there the same night. It was a night made for history; it was the first time Seamus had performed in the Millennium in Derry (amazingly!); the first time the Fleadh was held in Derry. Through the music and poetry the atmosphere was mystical.

Immersed in the poetry and music, I realised it was the most spiritually awakening experience I had in years. Little did I know then that it would be one of the last public appearances made by the Nobel Laureate; the last time I would hear his unique solemn reading of his own magnificent works of art. I shall treasure the memory forever.

On that night there was a real sense of vulnerability in the poet, especially as he recited in his distinctive soft voice: 'You are neither here nor there, / A hurry through which known and strange things pass / As big soft buffetings come at the car sideways / And catch the heart off guard and blow it open.' ('Postscript')

Three of Heaney's poems have propped up my spiritual life for decades. I came to him through Patrick Kavanagh – the first poet I really understood, who highlighted the deep significance of the apparently insignificant. Heaney, himself, acknowledged that he found in Kavanagh, 'details of a life that I knew intimately'.

Seamus Heaney's universally known 'Mid-Term Break', which he wrote in a bedsit ten years after his brother Christopher's tragic death, made me cry when I first read it. It has done so many times since, when I helped parents to bury their children in little white coffins. I prayed it nightly after my five-year-old nephew died. Tears rolled down my cheeks when Seamus Heaney read it that night in the Millennium, in the certain knowledge that it will have the same power to 'blow open my heart' every time I pray it.

That was when I recognised Heaney's miraculous ability to knock you sideways with a last line that slides in, bringing the poem to a stunning end while simultaneously creating a new beginning of a lifelong, personal, reflective search for meaning.

When my mother died at an age when she and I were young, I wish I had known his wonderful sonnet 'When all the others were away at Mass'. How such an ordinary chore as a mother and son peeling potatoes could become a symbol of warmth and love is the mysticism of poetry.

By the time my father died suddenly, I was lucky enough to be familiar with 'The Follower'.

All those evenings I spent working beside my father in the bog spreading and clamping turf; all the back-breaking summer nights weeding potatoes – and every other vegetable that would thrive in mossy ground – were summed up perfectly by Heaney. I wondered how he knew 'I was a nuisance, tripping, falling, / Yapping always. But today / It is my father who keeps stumbling / Behind me, and will not go away.'

There's that 'shocking' last line again.

I heard Seamus Heaney say in an interview that one of his greatest poems came as a gift almost. He and Marie, and Brian and Anne Friel, were driving in Co. Clare one especially windy day and stopped to look out over the bracing Atlantic Ocean.

The experience was mind-blowing and immediate. Later that evening he went to his room, wrote 'Postscript' and read it for his companions at dinner that evening.

And I hope these pages might encourage both you and I to make the time to 'drive out west', to escape and reflect on the beauty of life and God's creation. Then, we too will be able to experience what we need to experience – big soft buffetings coming at you sideways, 'And catch the heart off guard and blow it open.'

For it is only when the heart is broken open that we can know the need for healing.

As Valjean says in *Les Miserables*: 'You have love; that's the only future God gives us,' and further on he says, 'Love is the foolishness of men and the wisdom of God.'

I was thinking about how my parents arranged for me to be brought to the church, with godparents, and to be baptised in a font and made one of God's children. I often wonder though, if they had left me until I was twenty years of age would I have chosen to be baptised then? Would I do it now?

My answer is I hope I would, but I am not sure. To do so I would need to know that baptism would give a specific meaning to my life that it would provide me with the hope and courage to overcome the darkness of the journey in this world. I would need to be convinced of the beauty of the gift that baptism is.

I would need to accept that being a member of the church is a good and necessary thing. I would need to appreciate the value of community and the challenge to work for justice. I would need to see the church as life-giving.

I would need to see that baptism leads me to a life with Christ. It proves to me that there is more to life than what I see, than what meets the eye, on this earth. I would need to see that life is a journey with and to God and that I am a child of God.

And lastly, I would need to understand that I am loved by God; no matter what I think of myself, God always loves me. That love is at the centre of all our religion and ritual.

The 'Word made Flesh' is God's greatest gift to all people of goodwill. It is not just available to the chosen people or the special people. The Magi, or wise men, represent all those who seek the light and are of good faith. St Paul makes it very clear when he says: 'Pagans share the same inheritance; they are part of the same body and the same inheritance.' Nobody now can succeed in keeping God a captive or a prisoner in their way of thinking or indeed their church. Salvation comes to people all over the known world because the wise visitors represent the ends of the earth seeking God and finding him.

The feast of the Epiphany is the story of light overcoming darkness. The wise travellers came from all the nations and followed their star which led them to a safe place of hope. They represent the wisdom of all nations who had the courage and the hope to follow their dreams. The message to us is that we should *not* let the darkness of life take away our hope. These travellers were wise because they walked to the light and they trusted that God would overcome all evil. Epiphany for them and for us is the light that overcomes the darkness.

People in authority tend to kill dreams because they can be dangerous and threatening. They wish to destroy our vision but the message is that we should not deliver ourselves to them – we should avoid them. We should make sure to protect ourselves so that they can never kill our spirit.

Life is a constant search for meaning. But when we take the risk of journeying in search of God, we discover that those same journeys are filled with little epiphanies which enlighten the way for us.

We too should try to discover the light of Christ within our lives.

Gifts given generously will lead to a transformation in ourselves and in those with whom we share our gift.

I am reminded of a story about a Passionist friend of mine in America who is an only child. His elderly father was two thousand miles away from where the priest lived and was in the last days of his life because of cancer.

When the priest went to his father's room, he did what we all do – he prayed unceasingly and offered Mass for his father. The nurses in the care home called him aside one day and said to him: 'We know that you are doing your best by being a good priest to your father. But actually your father doesn't need a priest. He's had all the priests he needs in his life. What he does need is a son and you are the only one he has got. So stop being a priest and start being a son. That's what would really help him to leave this life. Give him permission to go.'

So he approached his father in one of his lucid moments to explain to him that he had lived a long life; told him that he was a wonderful father and he thanked him for all the sacrifices he had made. And it was time now for him to go to heaven and spend an eternity with mum.

The old man thanked his son and said he was very glad to hear that. He also told his son that he had enough money saved to rent an apartment for a year should the son ever feel the need to leave the priesthood. The man went to sleep and died within the hour.

The son realised that he had come to help his father to die, but that his father had given him an even greater gift, he gave him permission to live. He gave a gift to his father that his father graciously accepted and the father in turn gave his son an even greater gift: the permission to start life all over again.

Jesus came back to his own hometown and was such a celebrity that he was invited to preach in the synagogue on the Sabbath. Jesus was handed a scroll, since there were no books at that time. It contained the Book of Isaiah and Jesus knew that there was one beautiful passage in that which was a mission statement for what the Messiah should be like:

> The Spirit of the Lord has been given to me
> For his has anointed me
> He has sent me to bring good news to the poor.
> To proclaim liberty to captives
> And to the blind new sight
> To set the downtrodden free
> To proclaim the Lord's year of favour.

This is how the Messiah will live and act and he will not be the kind of Messiah they are expecting. This Messiah will not be politically powerful but he will mix with the marginalised and the outcasts of society, the very people who are looked down on by his orthodox listeners.

Whatever our poverty is Jesus will meet us in our poverty rather than our plenty. Poverty, of course, refers to the poor of this world but it also applies to the poor in spirit and to our own inner vulnerability. We are loved in our poverty.

He will bring freedom to the captives. Whatever it is that imprisons us, Jesus, if we trust him, will bring us freedom. The most difficult prison to escape from is the prison we impose upon ourselves through prejudice, bigotry and narrow-mindedness. Maybe the greatest prison is that of not wanting to be disturbed. Not wanting to change. Jesus can bring freedom only to those who are willing to move on, to change, to be challenged and to journey to a vulnerable place.

The poet W. H. Auden, writing in 1948, when the world was still slowly recovering from the catastrophe of war, observed:

> We would rather be ruined than changed.
> We would rather die in our dread
> Than climb the cross of the moment
> And let our illusions die.

That is how so many of us imprison ourselves unnecessarily. We'd rather be ruined than be changed. What a powerful description of so many official churches today. They would rather be ruined than be changed.

Sometimes we, in our preaching and in our devotion to the Passion, concentrate too much on the physical punishment of Jesus. The gospels do not dwell on, or highlight, the physical suffering of Jesus. They mention it almost in passing, and to make a theological point.

We look at Jesus hanging on a cross and there we see the model of what the church should be. Jesus is silent – his hands and feet nailed to the cross. He gives his last drop of blood for us and tells us that for a Christian, real power is found in powerlessness. Jesus is never comfortable with show and pomp.

Rather than the physical suffering of Jesus, we begin to recognise both our strengths and our weaknesses. We realise that:

- Judas is not the only one who betrayed a friend.
- Peter is not the only one who protected himself and was willing to deny others to do so.
- The religious leaders who put Jesus to death were not the only religious leaders who abandoned innocent victims so that they could protect their own reputation and institution.

We need to be careful not to get carried along by the crowd.

I am reminded of a wonderful quotation from Martin Luther King: 'At the end of the day it is not the words of your enemies that you remember; it's the silence of your friends.'

We recognise our strengths and our weaknesses in the reliving of the suffering, death and Resurrection of Jesus, our Saviour.

Jesus rose from the dead and is present here among us. That's what we believe. We meet the risen Jesus in the signs of the times. We will meet the risen Jesus in people willing to risk their life hungering for peace or struggling for justice – people who hear the cry of the poor, the oppressed and victims everywhere.

The risen Christ is evident in the compassion and sacrifice it takes to bring about a better world. That is the promise of Christ in Matthew 28:20: 'I am with you always until the end of time.' Christ lives and will be with us until the end of time, in the lives of Christians who continually rise with him each day.

We recognise the risen Jesus when we allow ourselves to come out of our tombs of apathy. Jean Vanier said: 'We must learn to rest in that peace which comes when God touches our hearts – that peace is the presence of God. That's how God speaks to us.'

Faith is a journey. For some on a journey they have a need for signs to get them there. Others don't; they seem to have a built-in satnav. But the gospel says both are blessed. Blessed are you who have seen and believed. Blessed are you who have not seen and yet believe. Both are blessed.

Doubt is not an obstacle to faith; it is part of faith's journey. Jesus says to Thomas: 'Touch my wounds and believe.' He is also telling us to touch our own failures and our own woundedness. He is telling us to have peace and forgive ourselves and believe that God loves us. Thomas had doubts and Jesus accepted his prayer and led him through it. As Thomas Merton puts it so beautifully: 'A person without doubt is a person without faith.'

I was at a play in a theatre in Leicester Square, London. On the way out from this inspiring drama, I was feeling truly elated. Then as I turned into the tube station, I noticed, and almost walked past, a young girl sitting on the ground with her dog, collecting money.

It was a freezing cold night. I went back to her and spoke to her; she had a Scottish accent. I gave her a few pounds and I advised her to give up collecting and get herself some hot food. She smiled and seemed genuinely grateful.

Just as I walked away another couple came out of the theatre and stopped. A well-dressed lady stooped down and petted the dog. She talked for two or three minutes to the dog but never said a word to the young woman. And then she straightened up and said to her husband: 'The dog seems well cared for.' They went on their way, content.

Simon Peter made many mistakes. The Lord asked him to walk on water and he made a complete mess of it. He let Jesus down on the night before his death when he could not manage to watch one hour with him. Later on, he denied that he ever knew Jesus – this same friend who had washed his feet and given him an example of how to live; the same friend who had left the sustaining food of his Body and Blood to the community. When Peter warmed himself at a fire and denied that same friend, the fire obviously did nothing to warm his cold feet.

We have a God who is more interested in our future prospects than he is in our past failures. That's the new life and that's the hope of the Resurrection.

I was in a religious bookshop and I noticed a book by Frederick Buechner. He's a writer I like and I was struck by the following quote: 'When you confess your sins to God, you are not telling God anything he doesn't already know.'

Maya Angelou gave a perfect summary of a vocation once: 'People will forget what you said, people will forget what you did, but people will never forget how you made them feel.' I've often used that as an examination of the way I do things myself. I think it is a powerful way of discovering whether I do a job or just provide a service.

'Peace I bequeath to you; my own peace I give you; a peace the world cannot give, this is my gift to you. Do not let your hearts be troubled or afraid.' The special gift Christ gave to all who saw him after the Resurrection was the gift of peace. And it is the gift given to all who experienced the risen Lord in any way.

It's interesting that Jesus says: 'Do not *let* your hearts be troubled.' I think that's significant. Nobody can steal your peace unless you give them permission. The advice Jesus is giving us is that we should not *let* them steal our peace. Jesus tells us: 'My peace I give you.' So it's not just any peace. It's a special gift from Jesus himself. He is reassuring us that when the special peace he gives us is ours, then we should not let anyone take it away. Our peace is a gift from God and God alone; we should not let anyone take it from us.

The preface of the Mass of the Ascension says: 'Jesus is the mediator between God and human beings. He has ascended into heaven not to distance himself from us, but so that we might follow where he has gone.'

That in essence means that we now have to be the physical presence of Jesus on earth. We have no other way of showing his compassion other than through us and our actions.

I came across a little piece of poetry which says:

I am my neighbour's Bible; he reads me when we meet.
Today he reads me in my house, tomorrow in the street.
He may, a relative or friend of slight acquaintance be,
He may not even know my name, yet he is reading me.

After Jesus ascended to heaven, we find the disciples locked behind closed doors in absolute fear. They allowed their fear to cut them off from the world. They were locked behind closed doors yet the Holy Spirit broke in. As soon as they experienced the Holy Spirit their fear disappeared and instead they were filled with joy and peace and love and new life. So why do we allow ourselves to become prisoners of fear?

Donal Walsh, the sixteen-year-old boy from Kerry who died from cancer in 2013, after a four-year struggle with the disease, lived hope every day in spite of his illness. It was his plea to those who contemplated taking their lives by suicide that had the biggest impact. He wrote: 'Life is precious. I was given no choice, no say in the matter; yet I hear teenagers talking of suicide as a way to solve their problems. As a sixteen-year-old with no choice in the death sentence I received, or indeed no choice about the pain I am about to cause my mother and father, family and friends; and I know I would do anything for a few more months of life on this planet; I urge you to appreciate what you have, to know that you have other options than taking your own life, and realise that help is always there.'

Elizabeth Johnson is an insightful American theologian who understands that mysteries are not puzzles to be solved and that we need to learn to live with mystery in a fulfilling way. To speak of the Trinity is not to come face-to-face with an insoluble puzzle – it is to have some sense of the wonder of God's presence.

In a healthy spiritual life, God is at the centre of every moment. *I* have to move aside to allow God's creative work to continue.

God sees within each of us a masterpiece that we cannot see ourselves. God sees the masterpiece in the damaged, broken lives of each one of us and that is what makes all the difference. Trinity is in fact the sculptor who takes the messiness of our lives and creates the masterpiece that God always intended us to be. That's the power of the love of God, the root of life, the saviour and giver of all life.

It is true what they say – when the elderly die, they take much of our past with them; but when the young die they take part of our future with them. In the gospel stories, we hear about Jesus restoring a dead son to his mother. Our reality means we have to live with death as part of the human condition. In the midst of death and sadness, we have to bring life out of these tragic situations in a different way.

We do this by attempting to have the same compassion as Jesus had, by bringing life to tragic situations. Compassion often brings life to those who mourn. We cannot divert tragedy or sadness, but we can be present in it, accompanying those who are bereaved.

To do this, we need to be aware of the brokenness and vulnerability in those we meet. We need to give them time and a listening ear to share their vulnerability. To do it effectively, means we have to be aware of our own vulnerability and brokenness. We need to move aside so that God can work through us. That is the only help and compassion we can bring that is healing or worthwhile.

Two million children die each year of hunger. One in eight people does not have enough food to have a healthy life.

Gandhi said we have to look into our hearts to bring about change in a just way. His words were: 'You must be the change you wish to see in the world.'

We can't simply pray for those who suffer, without being aware of our own responsibilities for some part of that suffering.

Life changes who I am and who you are. Who I am now is different from who I was twenty or thirty years ago. And if I am still a child in a man's body then life has passed me by.

Equally, my answer to the question 'what is God like?' should change with the years. They say growing old is mandatory, growing up is optional. There are people who never change and that is, sadly, a wasted life.

Jesus has many faces. When he was with Martha and Mary, he was a quiet man, in need of intimacy, friendship and understanding, with good food and good friends; he was at peace. When he went to the Temple and found people desecrating the holy place, he flew into a rage. In the Transfiguration he was indeed the face of God. On the cross he was the face of despair.

The lesson is to accept who we are, as we are; we continue to remember that we are on a journey; that we are not perfect and that we don't have to be perfect. God accepts us as we are and as long as we try to be the best we can be then we are on a good journey, constantly changing, constantly getting to know God as the giver of all gifts and constantly getting to know ourselves as one who couldn't exist without those gifts.

Nelson Mandela said that if he reached the gates of heaven he would first ask if Oliver had got in. Oliver Tambo was one of the inspirational leaders in the African National Congress (ANC), who died violently. If Oliver was there he would enter, then seek to find out where Hitler was. And if he found Hitler washing floors then he would know he had arrived in heaven. The idea being, he said, that heaven should be a place where dictators and tyrants are humbled. An interesting vision of heaven, that.

It is a constant theme of scripture that to be a follower of Jesus, we must live the consequences of that choice. Elisha talks about following the Lord and needing time to leave his parents to be a disciple of the prophet Elijah. But then he is warned that he must make a total commitment. He decided to follow the prophet. He not only left home but smashed the tools of his trade. There would be no turning back.

The option is a simple one in biblical terms. We either stay the same or serve God – one or the other – we cannot do both.

Is this, for example, a good or a bad time to be a Catholic? We are like a remnant of the past. We can choose to gather up the fragments and save what we have. Or we can acknowledge that God's call is to something unknown and life-giving. Jesus looks for people who will walk with him and live his teachings anew rather than choose the safety of slow death.

Martin Buber, the Jewish philosopher, said: 'Nothing so much masks the face of God as religion.' Religion can be an addiction in itself, based on duty. It can become a burden and without joy.

We have to accept the God of Love. Despair, they say, is not necessarily a loss of faith, but simply a lost memory of how good God has been to us. And that's what we're asked to be and live today.

Discipleship, following Christ, is not for the faint-hearted. It is a choice we make. We live it out daily in our lives. Ernest Hemingway wrote: 'It is good to have an end to journey towards; but it's the journey that matters in the end.'

It is easy to put our hand to the plough and be tempted to turn back. We do not know where life will lead us. Much of it we cannot control. We have to accept what comes our way on the journey and make choices because of that. But we do have to change and be different. Daniel Berrigan, the iconic Civil Rights leader, believed, 'The best way to make the future different is to live the present differently.' We cannot go on doing things in exactly the same manner and hope to achieve a different result. If we continue to do things as we always did, we're likely to get the same results we always got. Rather, we have the opportunity to live differently now to determine how we can make the future different.

Being a disciple is a call to live differently and to live graciously in this world. Jesus appoints every disciple of every time and place to go before him and to be agents of compassion, reconciliation and hope to a needy world. John XXIII, some days before he died, said: 'I believe that when I stand before God, God will simply ask me: How did you use the gift of life I gave you?'

It is important to recognise that nobody was really condemned in the story of the Good Samaritan. But people had questions to answer not for what they did, but for what they failed to do. The whole story is an answer to one simple question: 'And who is my neighbour?' This question of 'Who is my neighbour?' is a real prickly one. We don't choose them. We have to discover who they are.

The Good Samaritan is the embodiment of what Christ wants Christians to become. Somebody once said that our hell will be when on the last day of life the person we are met by is the person we could have become.

We don't think ourselves into new ways of living; we live ourselves into a new way of thinking. I remember a woman coming to confession many years ago who was annoyed with a sermon I had preached, in which I said that people in second relationships should find a place in the church. She interpreted this as an attack on Christian marriage. We agreed to differ. Many years later she came to me again. By now her eldest daughter's marriage had broken up. She had met another man who was extraordinarily good to her. The mother had changed her mind, now saying that the church was too harsh not to give people a second chance. She could never have thought herself into that position. But as she lived life, it changed her into a new way of thinking.

Hospitality is a theme that runs right through the Bible. The Old Testament regarded hospitality as an essential virtue. In those days, every visitor could be seen as a potential enemy. The rule of hospitality helped to overcome this suspicion of people. All decent people should offer hospitality to whoever comes their way; they should not be suspicious of them. If it is accepted graciously and if gratitude is shown for the hospitality, that becomes the basis of a future relationship. Hospitality opens the door to friendship and relationships – a wise principle, indeed.

In the New Testament, we see an interesting development of hospitality. When Jesus visits Mary and Martha, Martha fulfils the traditional understanding of hospitality with the provision of seating and food. Martha's hospitality is genuine discipleship. But Mary sits at the feet of Jesus. A rabbi was not supposed to talk to or teach a woman. They were not worthy! Yet, Jesus makes it clear that Mary is to 'sit at his feet' and to continue sitting at his feet. That phrase is important. 'To sit at the feet' of the rabbi was to be a disciple and be taught by the rabbi. So even though women were not thought worthy of an education, Jesus breaks all taboos and affirms Mary as a disciple. She recognises this is a special moment in her life, a graced moment. That is when she knows she has 'chosen the better part'. Martha was a genuine disciple and Mary was a faithful disciple. Jesus affirms that both hospitality and listening are services, but he also highlights that commitment to Jesus is central to discipleship. That's 'the better part'.

We are called to be hospitable, that is, to be open to others when they come. Not just to put up with them but to be open to their life story. That openness should spring from commitment to Jesus. It leads to a prayerful relationship with Jesus, which of course is to our advantage.

In a sense, Martha has a list of things 'To Do'. Mary's list is a reminder of what our vocation 'To Be' is. It is not enough for us to be *among* people, we have to actually *be* with them.

'God's work always begins with listening.'

Richard Rohr, the great modern spiritual writer, said: 'When you pray, pray in, not up.' Prayer is about perseverance. Not pestering God to get our way, but perseverance until we're open enough to know where God is leading us, and we are willing enough to accept the strength from God to fulfil it.

Prayer is not just about words. We become our prayers. Genuine prayer begins with gratitude. Every breath we take. Every step we take. Every moment we have in existence. Everything that is good and difficult and wonderful and sad in our lives is a gift from God. We cannot even breathe without being grateful to God for that. Prayer begins with gratitude that we are here in this place and that God is still with us.

Prayer is talking *with* God, not talking *to* God. And even more importantly prayer is listening to God. Which of these is the better way of describing your attempts at prayer?

a) Speak Lord, your servant is listening.

b) Listen Lord, your servant is speaking.

If you can answer that question honestly, you will see it is not so much me talking to a God who does not listen, it is much more God talking to me who has not learned to hear.

A quotation often used by Richard Rohr is: 'You never know that God is all you need until you realise that God is all you have.'

The poet Alan Jones said: 'There is a self in each of us waiting to be born.' No matter how long we live there is something new to discover about our own selves. There is a self in each of us which has been suppressed. There is a self in each of us waiting to be born.

The American poet Maya Angelou explained in a conversation with *Time* magazine: 'Imagine if we were not crippled by these idiocies of prejudice, sexism, and racism …there is still hope …. There is hope and sometimes you need to be jarred into finding it. Believe in something in your life – so fervently that you will stand up with it until the end of your day … I hope for that. I write for that. I speak for that, I sing about that, I pray about that.'

Pious law-keepers of religion condemned Jesus roundly for healing a man on the Sabbath. Jesus healed him because he was sending out a message they had difficulty receiving: that compassion and care for the person is more important than hiding behind the law.

So look at your life today. Be gentle with yourself but also be real. What are the important issues in your life? What do you hope for? What sort of church do we hope for in the future, when the hard lessons are properly learned?

Jesus warns those following him not to make religion mere show. Rather, 'Try your best to enter by the narrow door because I tell you many will try to enter but will not succeed.' The narrow door is open to everybody, but it will be those who live honestly who enter it. There is no automatic entry as if we were members of some special club.

I came up with four areas of my life to use as a test whether I am living a proper life or not, looking at what I do and what I should do in the light of what Jesus taught.

1. We have to lead an honest life with integrity. We need to know that our life is not a sham. Of course there will be times when there will be hypocrisy in our lives. But if our whole life is just about the external show then it is a sham.

2. We must have an active concern for the poor. Reading the gospels, it is absolutely clear that unless the poor are a priority for us then we are not living gospel values. We cannot claim to be Christian unless we help the poor in a radical way. It is not just the poverty-stricken, but also the neglected; those who endure poverty of education and poverty of opportunity. We must fight, *really* fight, for justice for them.

3. We must be part of a community. Communion at Mass indicates that as each of us receives the Body of the Lord Jesus, we are in communion with him and in communion with one another. Communion is impossible without community. We cannot go to God as a stand-alone individual. We have to contribute to the community and depend on the community to pray for us and with us. We have to generously offer our gifts to the community.

4. We must have peace and compassion at the centre of our lives. There is, as it were, a 'good spirit' and a 'damaging spirit' within each of us. Whichever spirit we feed will dominate us. We have to ensure the good spirit within us is developed. It is not just enough to be compassionate. I think it was Fr Peter McVerry who said that we have to 'Be the compassion of God.' Unless I act in a compassionate way on behalf of God, to a person in need, then that person is deprived of God's compassion. Each of us has to be the compassion of God to those in need.

Another biblical theme worth thinking about is humility. We have gifts but we have received them from God. We are encouraged to get the proper perspective on life in a genuinely humble way. We are not asked to play down our gifts, but to recognise that they come from God, and without God we have nothing.

Instead of jockeying for seats of honour at a banquet, the followers of Jesus are to take the lowest place and leave the giving of honour to the discretion of the host. The human ego could easily convert this instruction about humility into a new strategy for self-aggrandisement. Taking the lowest seat out of humility is one thing; taking the lowest seat as a way to move up is another. Jesus was not giving his disciples a gimmick for self-promotion. It reminds me of a prayer a young man, having difficulty with religion, had pinned to his wall. It said: 'O Lord lead me towards those who seek the truth – but deliver me Lord from those who have found it.'

How might society be affected if the followers of Jesus allowed humility to uproot our arrogance, anger, greed and aggression, our excess of pride and ambition? With our feet on the ground and our eyes fixed on Jesus, we are challenged to be truly who we are at all times, in all places, with everyone we meet.

Autumn is a time to let go with dignity. The leaves will fall and they will fertilise the land. Falling leaves will remind us that we have to let cherished things go. We have to trust God that this is one of the many cycles of life. The beautiful summers, the deaths of autumn. The coldness of winter, the new life of spring. It gives us an opportunity to trust God and to let things go graciously.

The leaves falling represent the cherished things in life that have to change. Nothing stays the same. Leaves are like the losses we have in life. There is a connection between what dies and what grows out of the death. It could be the loss of a job, the loss of money, the loss of status, the loss of a home or the loss of a relationship. These are all like falling leaves. No matter how we resist them they happen, but if we accept them and make peace with them, we can grow to be different and better people.

If you are lost and vulnerable and feeling forgotten, take hope today because God knows the value of one. God knows the value of the lost one. When the lost one was found there was a plea to 'Rejoice with me.' Rejoice with me for finding the lost sheep and the lost coin and, indeed, the lost son. Not even the begrudging son, who never did anything wrong, was listened to. He was told that if he never did anything wrong perhaps he might not have done much right either, but that God would save him anyway. And if God saved him what right had he to complain when others were saved by God's generous love?

In the last week of September 2013, in interviews with some Jesuit magazines, Pope Francis said: 'The church has locked itself in too many small-minded rules.' He went on to say that the most important ministry of the church is the proclamation of the gospel, which is the good news that Jesus Christ has saved you. How strange that this should make headlines. What else should a pope say? He also said: 'Ministers of the Church must be ministers of mercy.' Again why is this news? Jesus said it frequently in the gospels. The pope went on to tell us that priests should 'walk with people'. We should help them as the Good Samaritan helped his neighbour. And once again we see the source of it all: the gospel. How did this message of Jesus become so distorted within the leadership of a church meant to represent him, that it now makes world headlines?

The pope said: 'The church, if it doesn't change, will collapse like a house of cards.' Funnily enough, that is one of the statements that was attributed to me and which led to the letter of censure from the Roman Curia, along with the threat of excommunication.

Finally, he said: 'The church has a home for *all*. Not just a small chapel of select people.'

Yet, these sensible words from Pope Francis evoked a great sadness in me. Only one year prior to his comments, the BBC was preparing to run a documentary on me with the title *The Turbulent Priest*. From the documentary it was clear that I said, and kept saying for the last ten years, almost exactly what the pope said those interviews. And all the people who were congratulating the pope, especially particular priests and Catholic journalists, were the very people who wrote that if I held those views I should leave the Catholic Church and join some other religion.

Other priests saying similar things to me were also treated in the same disparaging way. Now within a very short space of time these clerical and lay commentators have changed their minds – and most of them say they felt it was long overdue for the leadership of the church to say these things. Even Pope Francis' statement that the church has a home for all and not just a select few, was vigorously challenged by the Curia little more than a year previously.

It is good that the Roman attitude has changed but it is sad that so many people had to suffer so much. And what is slightly perturbing is how this 'new thinking' has been so readily embraced by those who condemned it in other people only a short time ago. If Pope Francis' eventual successor (and I hope that's a long way off) takes a more restricted, more ultra-conservative, more clerical view, will all those praising Francis for his openness, suddenly do an about-turn? Is to be seen openly in agreement with the pope, regardless of what he is saying, the measure of a loyal follower?

The pope has told us that he himself has been reprimanded for his statements. So if these people are reprimanding the pope I suppose I should not wonder that others have been reprimanded too. Maybe it's part of gospel living.

I believe that the Holy Spirit recognises the truth and will create a time and space for the truth to come out. The gradual taking away of unnecessary layers is a true sign of the Spirit at work.

If we are too comfortable to notice the poor then we are in trouble. A couple of years ago I went to a meeting in the Barnabas centre in Enniskillen to discuss the possibility of setting up a new complex which might help young teenagers who are homeless in Fermanagh. I would consider myself to be alert to such needs. Yet when I asked the group, who are doing fantastic work, if there were many young homeless in Fermanagh, I was shocked to discover there are officially about forty young boys and girls – teenagers – who are officially registered as homeless. There are forty young people in Fermanagh who cannot stay in the family home for all kinds of reasons. It brought it home to me that I am like the rich man in the gospel. I think I am noticing everything but I certainly did not notice those homeless poor being housed by charities and the state. And this is not just a problem in Fermanagh, every county in Ireland has its homeless young people.

The gospel reminds us that thinking other people's lives are 'none of our business' is a false attitude.

As Carl Jung put it: 'You are what you do, not what you say you'll do.'

We should never underestimate the value of one. We need to understand that we might not be able to save the whole world. Nor are we asked to. But we are asked to help the person nearest. And that in itself is helping to save the whole world.

Oskar Schindler, whose actions during World War II were dramatised in the film *Schindler's List*, was given a gold ring, made from the dental bridgework of one of the workers of his factory. It was inscribed with a verse from the Talmud (the Jewish book of laws and rabbinic teachings): 'He who saves one life, it is as if he saved the entire world.'

Gratitude is more important to the person offering gratitude. It is an awareness of our own vulnerability. It is being humble enough to recognise that I need help; when I make myself vulnerable help is given. That is a life-changing form of gratitude and is much more than merely saying thank you.

Faith is a gift. It is a gift that should change the way we live and the way we live should help others in their search for meaning in life. Faith is something we share. This means that we try to help others and that we are, just as importantly, open to receiving something from others in return.

The activist Dorothy Day, towards the end of her life, said: 'Please don't dismiss me so easily,' when people began to speak of her as a saint. She realised that people regarded saints as something different, something special, and therefore what they did was not achievable for 'ordinary' people. What she did with her life is achievable for everyone if we are dedicated enough.

Day, an American woman, was a Communist who became a Catholic. She was a single parent and not overly religious in the pious meaning of the word. But she decided to help the poor. She dedicated her life, through the Catholic Worker Movement and the Dorothy Day Centres, to feeding the poor in cities right across America. She was once asked why she wasted her life on the poor, the addicted, and the mentally ill. She answered: 'I am here because *I* need them; I'm here because *I'm* hungry. People often say to me how nice it is to feed the poor. But I know in my heart that I am being fed by them. Christ is in and with the suffering and speaks to me through them.'

Jesus reached out to people across boundaries and to people on the margins. He offered healing, a chance to change their life and the opportunity of inner peace and fulfilment. Reconciliation was very much part of the way Jesus lived. Nobody was beyond help and nobody was beyond changing. I think that's what we need to concentrate on today.

Conor Cusack, a hurler from Cork, has written and spoken eloquently on his depression, near suicide and his recovery. He made quite a startling claim when he said: 'I came to realise that depression was not my enemy but my friend. I don't say this lightly. How can you say something that nearly killed you was your friend? The best coaches I have ever dealt with are those that tell you what you need to hear, not what you want to hear. You mightn't like it at the time but after or maybe years later, you know they were right.

'For those people who are currently gripped by depression, either experiencing it or are supporting or living with someone with it, I hope my story helps. There is no situation that is without hope, there is no person that can't overcome their present difficulties. For those who are suffering silently, there is help out there and you are definitely not alone.

'Everything you need to succeed is already within you. A good therapist will facilitate that process. The *real* you awaits within to be found but to get there requires a journey inwards. A boat is at its safest when it is in the harbour but that's not what it was built to do. We are the same.

'Your journey in will unearth buried truths and unspoken fears. A new strength will emerge to help you to head into the choppy waters of your painful past. Eventually you will discover a place of peace within yourself. The most important thing is to take the first step. Please take it.'

Jesus valued people more than rules. He reached out over boundaries of acceptability and he healed and restored. Belonging to Christ means that we risk reaching out when others will not.

Dr Rachel Naomi Remen is a master storyteller and a very successful author in America. She's also a cancer physician. She comes from the Jewish tradition. Her book, *My Grandfather's Blessings*, is about how we should recognise and receive blessings and bless life in others. She believes serving others heals us, as through our service we discover new depths within ourselves.

She tells how her grandfather gave her presents, but not the usual kind. One day he gave her a paper cup filled with clay and put it on her windowsill. She was only four years old, and was disappointed with this gift. But her father told her to put water in her toy teapot and water the clay in the paper cup every day. After a fortnight, the child, being so young, almost gave up. But her grandfather encouraged her to persevere. In the third week, she awoke to find two little green leaves. She could hardly wait for her grandfather's next visit, as she watched the leaves get bigger every day.

Of course, her grandfather was not surprised. He explained to Rachel that life is found everywhere, even in the most ordinary and unlikely places. When she suggested that all this life needed was water to be found, her grandfather gently explained that no, all the life needed was her faithfulness.

Rachel said that this was her first lesson in the power of service, even though her grandfather would not have used such words. He would have spoken about the 'need to remember to bless the life around us and the life within us. He would have said when we remember that we can bless life, we can repair the world'.

C.S. Lewis said: 'We are not *ordinary* people; we are not *mere* mortals; we are born to share the life of God.' He went on to say: 'Our challenge is that life is of immense costliness combined with the complete conviction that it is worth it.' His view was that to follow your vocation does not necessarily mean happiness; but once the call has been heard, there is no happiness for those who do not follow it.

Our vocations in life will be many and varied, but central to our Christian vocation is to make the kingdom of God real, here and now. The kingdom is made real when we learn by acts and not words – acts of kindness and compassion, acts of forgiveness and reconciliation. We *experience* a kingdom of truth, love, holiness, justice and peace. We *experience* a kingdom that belongs to the poor and the forgotten and the lost. We belong to a kingdom that has no boundaries. No matter which church excommunicates people, God's love never does.

Nelson Mandela is rightly revered as a man of peace. Yet, it was not always so. After Sharpeville in 1960 when thousands of black people were cruelly shot down as they protested against their treatment, Mandela believed that freedom would not be granted to the black people of South Africa 'like Manna from heaven'. They would have to fight for it. Those in power would not relinquish it voluntarily; it would have to be taken from them. In fact he agitated with the ANC Youth to overthrow the leadership of the ANC because they were too moderate. In a speech after his trial, he said he was prepared to die for his beliefs.

Archbishop Tutu was once asked if the twenty-seven years that Mandela served in prison were a waste of his life. Tutu said on the contrary it was during these years that Mandela became a leader. He entered jail as an angry young terrorist who wanted to use force against apartheid. But in true suffering he underwent a spiritual development; through reflection he learned to respect his enemies and to respect the fears of those in power.

He learned to live what he preached and especially he learned that unless we forgive and let go of bitterness we voluntarily waste our lives lost in the past. After he was freed he invited the man who was his jailer on Robben Island to be a VIP at his inauguration. Percy Yutar, who wanted him to be put to death, was invited to a special lunch and they later became friends. Mandela also backed the hated Springboks team (the film *Invictus* demonstrates his reasons for this).

Mandela knew that if you want to make peace with your enemy, you have to work with your enemy; then your enemy becomes your partner. And that is how a man who began as an angry young terrorist matured into a great world leader. It was the integrity of life and self-discipline which made him so.

As the Book of Proverbs says: 'A bird doesn't sing because it has answers; a bird sings because it has a song.' Each of us has to try to look for that song within ourselves and discover where it is.

On the day of Nelson Mandela's burial, I was thinking of a story from his book, *The Long Walk to Freedom*, about an African boy who brought his teacher a beautiful precious little shell as a gift. The teacher recognised that the shell was from a lake which was many, many miles away. So she was particularly grateful that the young boy had gone to the lake and brought back a shell. And she congratulated him and thanked him, saying you must have walked miles to get this shell. To which the boy replied: 'Teacher, the long walk is part of the gift.'

Sometimes we look back at the end of the year and we see nothing but failure in our life. But we have done good things and we have been in good situations. Become aware of what those are. We all make mistakes, because we are not perfect, because we are human. It is perfectly okay to be imperfect. If human nature was good enough for God to live in, surely it is good enough for each of us to live in, with all its imperfections. God loves us no matter what.

Recognise that you have much to be grateful for. A Cherokee Indian story says: 'When you were born, *you* cried and the world rejoiced; live your life so when you die, the *world* will cry and you will rejoice.'

I once got a Christmas card which showed a print of William Holman Hunt's famous painting, *Christ, Light of the World*. It depicts Jesus coming out of the dark holding a lantern which is dispelling the darkness. He arrives at a door and is about to knock on the door. The art critics of the time thought it was a brilliant but flawed picture. They highlighted the fact that Jesus was knocking at a door where there was no handle, no latch, no key. He was knocking at a door that couldn't be opened. William Holman Hunt had the last laugh when he explained that far from being a flaw, it was the central message of his picture. The point should have been obvious that when Jesus knocks he never forces his way in; the door must always be opened from the inside. The handle was inside the door. God brings us hope but we have to open the door to accept it.

The Word was made flesh and pitched his tent among us, and so, no matter what, God always accompanies us on the journey of life. God, quite literally, changes his address from heaven to earth. It is a reminder that we, too, need to be constantly on the move. We do so with confidence, assured of God's guidance on the road.

Do we really believe that God became one of us at all? Thomas Merton always claimed that some Christians do not actually truly believe in the Incarnation. We don't believe that God became human. We believe that Jesus was divine but that humanity was attached to him – not in a way that had any effect. That is not the way it is. God is fully human in Jesus. Merton said that if we believed that God was fully human we would have a greater respect for our own humanity. Perhaps that's a good question we might ask ourselves at Christmas: Do I think I have to become less human to become more holy? Is it not possible for me to be fully human, and the more fully human I become, the more holy I become and the closer to God I am?

Dorothy Day once said: 'I really only love God as much as I love the person I love least.'

This is an amazing statement. Think of the person you love least. Perhaps it is the person you wish you could get out of your life altogether. That is the extent of our love for God. It may seem harsh at first, but I am convinced it is also true.

Following Jesus is not about romantic cribs and Christmas trees, though they have their place in the celebration. It is about the hard choices in life, acknowledging our humanity so that we can, through our community, grow in love. As convinced believers, we do not have the luxury to choose whom we love. That is the difference between human love and God-like love.

The psychologist Carl Jung once said: 'Whether invited or not, God is always present.' Whether we recognise a God or not, God is in the events of our life, always giving us an opportunity to make choices that matter. Dr Martin Luther King Jnr wrestled with what God was pushing him to do. Shortly before he died he gave us a lovely insight into life. He said: 'Our lives begin to end the day we become silent about things that matter.'

The kingdom of God in gospel terms is not a place. The kingdom of God clearly is a way of being. We do not commit to a doctrine, but to following Jesus, if we read closely what the gospel says. We commit ourselves to following in the footsteps of Jesus, knowing that he will lead us to a good place and that as we walk with him, others may follow. We have to trust the Lord, which should not be difficult, but it is. Jesus recognises that the practice of religion can become a substitute for a relationship with God. Our relationship with Jesus is central and crucial. It is an experience of life. It is not simply following a doctrine.

Lao Tzu, a philosopher of ancient China, said: 'We shape clay into a pot, but it's the emptiness inside that holds what we need.' This image of clay in a potter's hand frequently describes a relationship with God in the Bible. We are clay in God's hands and he shapes each of us uniquely. All of us, though, are shaped to include a void and when we leave aside everything else, there is a great emptiness and space which we refill with even more useless 'treasures' until, when we are empty again, God finds a home.

It becomes easy for us in life to settle and lock ourselves into the past. We can lock ourselves into traditions and refuse to change or to trust or to believe. It is we who chose isolation. We can do it as people, as families, as companies and, most of all, as a church. Jesus, during the Resurrection story, puts it in a nutshell: 'Why look for the living among the dead.'

Look at what is dead in your life. Recognise it as a part of you to be left behind. Choose life; peace can never be present when we choose to live in the past and refuse to forgive. Note that in the gospel, after the gift of peace, Jesus tells the disciples that part of the good news will be that 'those whose sins you shall forgive are forgiven'. Forgiveness itself is part of this journey and this challenge. If I cannot forgive myself and if I cannot accept forgiveness from others, as well as offering forgiveness to others, then how can I live in peace?

The early Christian community recognised one special gift which set them apart: 'See how these Christians love one another.' Love is the hallmark of the Christian community. We see the wounded Christ in our own communities: in the vulnerability of children and the elderly; in courage; in living honestly and with integrity; in recognising compassion in kindness; in a smile from our neighbours; in the healing and forgiveness all around us. The disciples locked in the upper room regained their peace so that their fears disappeared when the spirit of the risen Jesus appeared.

A community or church which is more concerned with its own survival than the spreading of God's kingdom cannot be a true mission. A church which refuses to allow God to be as merciful and forgiving as God wishes, a church which refuses communion to people in difficulty – the very people who need it most – a church which drives people away from God rather than being an example of God's mercy, bears all the hallmarks of a failed institution. The criterion remains: 'See how these Christians love one another.'

Pope Francis believes that the church needs proper organisation but we must always let God be God. The church's mission is to spread God's kingdom. Pope Francis added: 'We, as Christians and we, as a church, should be dispensers of God's mercy not controllers of it.'

We are called to be committed Christians. It is often said that there are three kinds of people in society and three stages of commitment – or lack of it.

The first is a group of people who bury their heads and ignore the real world. They live in denial or, more properly, they die in denial because denial leads to death. They do not want to get involved in others' problems and so they live a solitary life, avoiding life really.

Secondly, there are those who take a grandstand view of everyone else's life and watch the world go by from afar. They are the hurlers on the ditch. They know what everybody else should do but they do nothing themselves. They can tell you where the government is going wrong, society is going wrong, where the churches are going wrong, but will they do anything to correct it? Not likely!

Thirdly, there are people who have enough conviction to roll up their sleeves and make things happen. That's what the gospel asks us to do. To be fervent, strong witnesses and to be people of conviction. God wants us to spread the good news by doing what the disciples were told to do – to preach, have faith and to do it with humility and compassion.

The Paradoxical Commandments are listed in a book by Dr Kent M. Keith called *The Silent Revolution*, published in 1968 to help young student leaders. In the forty-five years since, they have been used by leaders in a wide variety of fields to encourage people to keep going in the face of challenges. Mother Teresa even used them!

The Paradoxical Commandments

People are illogical, unreasonable, and self-centred.
Love them anyway.

If you do good, people will accuse you of selfish ulterior motives.
Do good anyway.

If you are successful, you will win false friends and true enemies.
Succeed anyway.

The good you do today will be forgotten tomorrow.
Do good anyway.

Honesty and frankness make you vulnerable.
Be honest and frank anyway.

The biggest men and women with the biggest ideas can be shot down by the smallest men and women with the smallest minds.
Think big anyway.

People favour underdogs but follow only top dogs.
Fight for a few underdogs anyway.

What you spend years building may be destroyed overnight.
Build anyway.

People really need help but may attack you if you do help them.
Help people anyway.

Give the world the best you have and you'll get kicked in the
teeth.
Give the world the best you have anyway.

I read about a twenty-six-year-old woman, Kayla Mueller. The news of her death while being held captive by the Islamic state devastated her family and friends. She was a young woman of extraordinary generosity and courage. Her family and friends remember her as the one who had a constant drive to make things better. After graduating from Northern Arizona University, Kayla worked with groups in Northern India, Israel and Palestine. She returned to Arizona in 2011 and spent a year working in a HIV / AIDS clinic.

The refugee crisis in Syria brought her back to the Syrian–Turkish border. During her time there, she dedicated her life to helping suffering people. 'For as long as I live I will not let this suffering be normal … it is important to stop and realise what we have, why we have it and how privileged we are,' she said.

Two months after those comments were published, Kayla herself disappeared while doing AIDS relief work.

God was very much part of her life. In 2011 she wrote to her father: 'I find God in the suffering eyes reflected in mine. If this is how you are revealed to me this is how I will forever seek you. I will always seek God. Some people find God in church. Some people find God in nature, some people find God in love. I find God in suffering. I've known for some time what my life's work is, using my hands to relieve suffering.'

In what was her final letter from prison in Syria, she wrote: 'I have been shown that in darkness there is light, and I have learned that even in prison one can be free … I have come to see there is good in every situation, sometimes we just have to look for it.'

Kayla refused to take an opportunity to escape so that another Western aid worker, an older woman with poor health, was not left on her own in prison. She embodied what it means to be a Good Shepherd.

The much-publicised fight between Floyd Mayweather and Manny Pacquiao earned the fighters approximately $210 million and $143 million, respectively. The total revenue raised through tickets, pay-per-view, advertising, sponsorship, etc., was more than $500 million.

Contrast that with the poor people of Nepal. There were more than eight thousand killed in an earthquake in the same week the fight took place. 2.8 million people have been displaced. Almost half a million houses were destroyed. Twenty-six hospitals were damaged. Kathmandu District has a population of 1.75 million in a land area of approximately 150 square miles. The historic buildings in the area have been destroyed and the livelihood of millions of people is in doubt as a result of it. Almost $90 million has been raised from donor countries around the world. And yet big businesses can raise $500 million for a boxing match.

I was reading the story of a famous, highly-regarded, Protestant theologian of the twentieth century, Karl Barth, who died in 1968. He had a huge influence on theologians of all ages, including those who were at the Second Vatican Council. He was once asked: 'What is the most important thought that ever entered your mind?' and after a brief moment of reflection, Barth replied: 'The most profound thought I have ever known is the simple truth, Jesus loves me, this I know, for the Bible tells me so.'

It is an amazingly simple, yet profound, insight from an internationally-renowned scholar, and it inspires me to sit quietly in gratitude.

Pierre Teilhard de Chardin was a Jesuit priest, a scholar, a scientist and deep thinker. He spent most of his adult life the subject of suspicion for the Vatican Curia. In 1929, in a letter to Fr Christophe de Gaudefroy, a French priest, he wrote:

'It has sometimes seemed to me there are three weak stones sitting dangerously in the foundations of the modern church: first, a government that excludes democracy; second, a priesthood that excludes and minimises women; third, a revelation that excludes, for the future, prophecy.'

That is a challenging insight from a unique philosopher who was no enemy of institutional religion. It is almost a century since he shared his insights and yet nothing has improved in the structure of the church. There is good evidence to show that the 'weak cornerstones' are causing the church to collapse.

God speaks to us through human prophets. It is impossible to 'resist the Spirit' and remain spiritually life-giving. In God's dealings with us, his people thrive when they are open to God's will and perish when they rely on their own resources.

This is a prayer for the beginning of a New Year – but it could also apply to any new direction in life we choose, or are forced to take, by circumstance or illness:

Lord in the New Year we have begun
May we have enough happiness to keep us agreeable
Enough trials to keep us strong
Enough sorrow to keep us human
Enough freedom to keep us happy
Enough failure to keep us humble
Enough success to keep us eager
Enough wealth to meet our needs
Enough faith to banish our depression
Enough hope to look forward
Enough love to give us comfort
And enough determination to keep us going.

There is a homeless centre in Galway and one year they exhibited works of art from the homeless on the theme of Christmas. One piece was painted on canvas in four little cartoon sections.

The first showed a small man down a hole. This hole represented being homeless, downtrodden or stuck in life. In this first section a doctor passes by and the man shouts: 'Help me, doctor.' The doctor thinks for a long time and writes a prescription and drops it down the hole and moves on.

The second section is a similar scene but this time it is a priest who comes by. 'Father, help me, I'm stuck in a hole.' The priest thinks, takes out his rosary beads, drops them down to him, blesses him and moves on.

The third passerby is a social worker, who drops some money and moves on.

The last section shows another homeless man, Murphy, and the man says: 'Hi Murphy, I'm stuck in a hole,' and Murphy jumps into the hole beside him. The man says: 'Now you have ruined everything, the two of us are stuck in a hole.' But Murphy says: 'Don't worry I've been down this hole before and I know the way out, follow me.'

Perhaps it's the strongest Christmas message you are going to hear. God joins us in our misery, walks with us and leads us to a better place.

Our faith calls us to choose light over darkness. To choose life and what is life-giving over that which sucks the very life out of us. Some people, through fear, envy and jealousy, tend to kill dreams because they feel threatened by them. It can be people in authority or people who pretend to be our friends. They wish to destroy our vision. But like the Magi, when we discover this, we must choose a different road to our destination. We should protect ourselves so that they do not damage our spirit.

Life is a constant search for meaning. But when we take the risk of journeying in search of God, we discover that those same journeys are also filled with little epiphanies which shine a light along the way for us. We should look for them and welcome them, for they come from the most unexpected of places.

Though we may be on the right road at the beginning of life, we need to constantly check that we can continue on the journey. Let us not forget that in life we are always free to choose a different future. But we cannot see change until we change the way we see. If you change your mind, you can change your life.

That possibility to change and grow for better or for worse is highlighted in a story about a man who was touring in Kerry. As often happens in Ireland there were not many signposts. He met a farmer on the road, who was on the way from Killarney to Kenmare, and the tourist asked: 'Am I on the right road to Kenmare?' The farmer looked at him benignly and said: 'You most certainly are on the right road to Kenmare, but you are going in the wrong direction.' Just being on the right road is not enough.

In St Luke's Gospel we read about Simeon, a devout man who, through the inspiration of the Holy Spirit, believed he would not die until he laid eyes on the Messiah. When Mary and Joseph presented Jesus in the Temple, as laid down in the law of Moses, Simeon was there, as was the prophet, Anna, an elderly woman.

As these two notable people began to speak about Jesus and praise God, Mary and Joseph were amazed. Jesus was their week-old baby, and they were still getting used to the impact a new baby makes on a family, especially the firstborn. Now they were being told that their baby, their precious newborn, was destined 'to be a sign that will be opposed so that the inner thoughts of many will be revealed – and a sword will pierce your own soul too'.

Babies rarely grow into the adults their parents had planned them to be. Yet, mostly, how they turn out is perfectly right for themselves. They must make their own journey.

Simeon and Anna were people of absolute faith and were rewarded in a way they appreciated. Mary and Joseph were shocked, yet remained faithful to the end. We know the journey Jesus took; he is the reason we still hope.

Oscar Romero used a lovely prayer which tells us we should be sensible in how we expect to grow.

'We plant seeds that will one day grow. We water seeds already planted, knowing that they hold future promise ... we cannot do everything and there is a sense of liberation at realising that. This enables us to do something and to do it very well ... we may never see the end result but that's the difference between a master builder and a worker – we are workers not master builders; ministers not messiahs; we are prophets of a future not our own.'

We should try to do something even though we can't do everything. Light a candle rather than curse the darkness.

The Book of Proverbs has many wise statements. One of which is: 'Where there is no vision, the people perish.' Sometimes within Christianity there is a tension between the value of law and the importance of love and this affects our vision of community.

Jesus left his people with a vision. It is important to remember that Jesus was, first and foremost, a good Jew. Many experts, including the foremost Catholic biblical scholars, conclude that there is no evidence that Jesus intended to form a religion separate from Judaism. A good Jew, during the time of Jesus, knew 613 laws and precepts off by heart and they formed the basis of a moral life. Jesus is not dismissing these laws but he is warning that they are not a vision in themselves. He has not come to dismiss them but to fulfil them and complete them.

How does he do this? By telling us that love goes beyond law. The law says that killing is forbidden. Jesus says the value behind this is that we should not let anger ruin our lives. Anger is a legitimate feeling and we must deal with it positively. If we don't it will destroy us and destroy others. The challenge for a Christian goes way beyond what the law says.

The law says: 'Do not commit adultery.' But a good Christian will recognise that this means respect for the gift of sexuality. That we do not let lust rule our lives. That we do not use sex as recreation. That we do not use people as objects for our own pleasure. The widespread availability of pornography is not an excuse to use it – just because it is there. It is important for us to recognise that the Christian approach is all about a positive appraisal of the gift of sexuality and not merely keeping the law.

We are asked to go beyond the surface and see the purpose of the law. We are to recognise that human beings are always more important than the law. And if keeping a law destroys a human being then don't keep it and don't destroy the human being. Follow the Spirit rather than the letter of the law.

Somebody once said that the hardest part of letting go is realising that there wasn't much to hold on to. 'If I'm holding on to something with both hands, I am unable either to give or receive.' We don't have much and therefore we want to hold on to the little we have. Jesus is saying, 'let go, lose control, commit yourself to love' and then you will understand the power of God working in your life.

In the Gospel of Matthew, we are told: 'You have heard it said, "You should love your neighbour and hate your enemy," but I say to you, love your enemies and pray for those who persecute you, so that you may be children of your Father in heaven.'

It is the exact opposite of what the world expects from us. The last verse of this gospel passage says: 'We are to be perfect as our heavenly Father is perfect.' Of course we now know that there is a more acceptable translation. It should read: 'Be compassionate as your heavenly Father is compassionate.' It's against our nature not to retaliate when insulted or to be non-violent. It's not normal that we put ourselves out for others and give as generously as the gospel wants us to do.

A counsellor once said to me: 'You can't hurt the feelings of a mature person; it's only the neurotic and the immature who take offence.' I wonder would many of us agree with that. Better still, I wonder are many of us gone beyond the neurotic and the immature. I doubt it, but it is an interesting discussion point.

A friend told me that he overcame alcoholism when he realised that he had to let go of bitterness and anger. He put it like this: 'To harbour bitterness is akin to swallowing poison and expecting your enemy to die.' (This quote is used in the AA manuals as part of the twelve-step programme.)

The Book of Proverbs has a wonderful saying: 'Ten enemies cannot hurt a person as much as a person who hates himself.'

J. R. R. Tolkien once described the choices we have to make and ended it with this sentence: 'All we have to decide is what to do with the time given to us.' We know that we cannot change the past, yet we can become so rooted in the past that it destroys a whole life. We idealise the past, recalling a time that never truly was as we choose to remember it. Or we remember only the suffering we endured, reliving the pain and the anger. So we are ruled from the past, either way.

Fear of change is the root of worry. We worry about the unknown and we worry about what we cannot control. Jesus acknowledges that there are parts of our lives which we should worry about. But the question he asks is: 'Can worry add a single hour to any life?' Tomorrow will take care of itself, the gospel tells us, and the most sensible statement of all: 'Each day has enough troubles of its own.'

St Augustine succinctly put worry in its place: 'Entrust the past to God; entrust the present to God's love; entrust the future to God's providence.'

Temptation is a complex experience which can be summed up as a false attraction which diverts us from our spiritual growth in life. If we are truly honest with ourselves, there are temptations we can foresee. The temptation to take the easy way out. The temptation not to let anybody stand in our way of achieving power, whether that is at a local, national or global level. The temptation to feed our greed and take what we think we deserve without consideration of the consequences.

There is a helpful way to examine our conscience each night by using the acronym SWOT. S = to look for our *strengths*. To thank God for them, and to cultivate them. W = to look and be aware of our *weaknesses*. To turn them into strengths and guard against falling under their power. O = *opportunities*. This is summed up in the Confiteor: 'I confess … in what I have done and in what I have failed to do.' Look for the opportunities which are given. What have I done with them and what have I not done with them. T = *Threats*. Where does the biggest threat come from? It could be from within or it could be from one of our weaknesses. We need to look at them honestly: our strengths, weaknesses, opportunities and threats.

We need not be disheartened by failure; as the psalm says: 'Our God is a God who seeks and saves that which is lost.'

All of us have to make journeys in life. Scott Peck, in his famous book *The Road Less Travelled*, summed it up in his one-sentence opening paragraph: 'Life is difficult.' And so it is. But we are not alone on our journey. If we are open to them, we will meet many people along the way who will inspire us, even transfigure us.

Archbishop Desmond Tutu once said that we should be 'transfiguration people'. That means we become a light to others by being true to ourselves. We should transfigure injustice into justice. We should transfigure condemnation into compassion. We should transfigure harshness into care, sorrow into laughter, despair into joy and hope. That's how each of us becomes the person we once needed to meet in our lives.

As the psalm tells us: 'May your love be upon us O Lord as we place all our hope in you.'

In our Novena of Hope held each year at the Graan, Enniskillen, the speakers who are invited are ordinary people who have experienced brokenness in their lives. I am glad they share their brokenness than any pious answers. They tell us how they struggled to survive, how they lived from day to day, and because of God's help and the help of neighbours and friends, they have made it this far. Hope is a slender but powerful thread.

The artist George Frederic Watts painted a picture in 1886 which he called *Hope*. It was to commemorate the death of a much-loved granddaughter. It is a dull-looking picture of a blindfolded woman clutching a lyre and sitting atop a globe. Three of the four strings of the lyre are broken and the woman appears to be listening intently to the single intact string as she plucks it. The painting attracted much negative comment at the time, with G. K. Chesterton suggesting that it should be called *Despair*. But Watts objected to this interpretation. He said: 'Hope need not mean expectancy. It suggests here rather the music which can come from the remaining chord.'

A copy of the painting was in Nelson Mandela's cell in Robben Island. Years later, a young black student heard a Baptist preacher tell the story of the painting at a Sunday service. That student had studied law and was about to join a firm which would have ensured his financial future. But when he heard the sermon from the preacher about this painting of *Hope*, he changed his mind and began to do social work helping his community, especially the black people in Chicago. If you go to the White House and enter the President's office you will find that there is still a copy of *Hope* on the President's desk, for that young lawyer was Barack Obama.

The story of the blind man in the gospel has much to tell us. The man was blind from birth, and in the ancient Near East, as well as in other cultures, sickness was often seen as punishment from God or the gods, either because of the deeds of the afflicted person or one or both of their parents. Jesus turned this understanding on its head. Not only did he heal the blind man, but did so on the Sabbath, which scandalised those who scrupulously kept the law.

The man born blind represents all of us. We do not know what is ahead of us. Sometimes people tell me it's just as well we don't know what is ahead of us because we would never face it. We have to live knowing that it is all in God's hands.

We can waste our lives worrying about why people suffer. The Pharisees believed that the man's bad life was the cause of his suffering. They had condemned him to sin, thereby making him worthless.

Jesus made him whole, healed him and led him from sin to faith. The point is that we should be more interested in helping those who suffer rather than wasting time worrying about the cause of suffering.

The blind man doesn't ask for healing. Jesus sees his need and offers it to him freely. The blind man was insightful enough to accept it. The religious authorities miss the point entirely. They are more concerned about control and good theology and good discipline than they are about healing, wholeness and what God wishes. The Pharisees saw the man as a sinner and dismissed him as useless. Jesus gave him a vision which he accepted. The Pharisees saw everything but understood nothing. The blind man saw nothing but had insight and vision.

Belief in Jesus and love for Jesus came *after* healing. The man didn't know who Jesus was. Jesus had to explain who he was.

God's love doesn't depend on faith or being perfect. God loves us anyway. The blind man when he experienced God's love accepted it.

Spirituality in life is the search for new vision and new sight. Sin is blindness. As St Gregory of Nyssa said: 'Sin is the refusal to grow.'

Those who know everything cannot learn anything.

The purpose of religious events such as missions, novenas and pilgrimages to well-known shrines is not to have a kind of mini drama festival of religion. Their purpose is to help us have a conversation about our way of living; to transform our way of living and to give us the grace and courage to be different. If we are not transformed, what is the point of such events?

A woman brought her twelve-year-old son to Mahatma Gandhi. The young son was causing great trouble in the home and had recently started to smoke. Gandhi looked at the mother and looked at the boy and asked them to come back after two weeks. The mother was disappointed but returned, as advised, two weeks later. Gandhi looked at the boy and said that he must start to behave better, that he should obey his parents and most of all he must give up smoking which is harmful to him.

The mother was delighted with what she heard, but wondered why Gandhi couldn't have said that two weeks previously. His answer was: 'Two weeks ago I myself was a smoker.'

The search for truth means that we live lives of integrity. We must lead by example and practise what we preach.

I came across this interesting opinion, written in the twelfth century by the Jewish philosopher Moses Maimonides.

He believed there are eight degrees of charity:

1. 'The first and the lowest degree is to give, but with reluctance and regret. A gift of the hand but not of the heart.' That one needs no explanation whatsoever.
2. 'The second is to give cheerfully but not proportionately to the distress of the suffering.' Like throwing a few bob in an envelope, or making a big deal over a small cheque. It was explained better by Mother Teresa: 'If you want to know the test of real charity, then you must give until it hurts.'
3. 'The third is to give cheerfully and proportionately but not until we are solicited.' In other words, if you can avoid being caught, avoid it. Never do anything until you are asked.
4. 'The fourth is to give cheerfully, proportionately and even when unsolicited but to put it in the poor man's hand, thereby causing him the painful emotion of shame.' Which means I wanted to give you this but I also want you to know how much it has cost me and where it came from, so that you'll feel under an obligation to me.
5. 'The fifth is to give charity in such a way that the distressed may receive the bounty and know their benefactor, without being known to him. Such was the conduct of some of our ancestors who used to tie up money in the back pocket of their cloaks so that the poor might take it unnoticed.'
6. 'The sixth, which rises still higher, is to know the object of our bounty but remain unknown to them. Such was the conduct of those of our ancestors who used to convey their charitable gifts into the poor people's dwellings taking care that their own persons and names should remain unknown.'

7. 'The seventh is better still, namely to give charity in such a way that the giver may not know the relieved persons, nor he the name of the giver.'

8. 'The best way of all, is to anticipate charity, by preventing poverty; namely to assist the needy brother or sister either by a considerable gift or a loan of money, or by teaching them a trade or by putting them the way of business, so that they may earn an honest livelihood and not be forced to the dreadful alternative of holding out a hand for charity. This is the highest step and the best charity of all.'

I suspect all of us have a few steps to climb yet.

The crowds welcomed Jesus by waving palm branches and laying their cloaks on the road before him. By the end of the week Jesus will be hanging on a tree alone and abandoned. This is a good time to ask ourselves some questions:

- At what point do we and Jesus part company?
- When does hope die?
- When do we drop the palm branches, pick up our cloak, and walk away?
- Is it when Jesus asks us to take up our own cross and follow him?
- Is it when he insists that we sell all we have and give to the poor?
- Is it when he tries to drag us out of our tombs that we have dug for ourselves where we feel safe from the evil of the world?
- Is it because there are too many questions asked of us and it is just a case of one more nice guy finishing last? One more deluded guy who fails? One more martyr for a cause we do not quite get?

Sometimes, we believe that Jesus was put to death by naked hate. He was not. He was put to death by everyday common vices that we all share, such as self-interest, indifference, fear, gossip, half-truths. The type of vices we rationalise our way through every day.

The ultimate measure of a man – or woman – is not where he stands in moments of convenience; but where he stands in times of controversy and crisis.

The only 'relic' I have from my mother now is a prayer book. It is a cheap leather-bound prayer book with large type. I recall coming home from school welcomed by a big roaring turf fire in the hearth. Kettles and pots bubbled and as often as not my mother would be leaning over a chair praying from her bulging prayer book.

Even then we used to laugh about the prayer book. It grew and grew as the years went by. It held cuttings from papers, special prayers that she had found in religious magazines, memoriam cards for neighbours and family. It was her file, her treasury and the most important book in her possession. Alongside it was her rosary beads and various prayers to be said. Her day was not complete until she had 'got through' her rituals.

To be part of mother's prayer book was to be remembered in a safe place. You would never be forgotten precisely where you shouldn't be forgotten. Over the years as it got plumper, an elastic band held it together.

Perhaps all of us collect emotional prayer books which are important memories from our past. We all have memories of faith, quiet joys that we not only remember, but which helped make us who we are.

The Resurrection story for early Christians is precisely that. It is a collection of faith memories which meant so much to those early Christians. They did not need proof that Jesus is risen from the dead. They knew it in their hearts. The Resurrection tells us that the last barrier between God and humanity is destroyed. God does not fail us and God's love is greater than all our human weakness.

If we believe that, we should live as if we believe it. We should live like Easter people who are full of hope and know that whatever befalls us God will take care of us, as he has until now.

Thomas recognises the resurrected Jesus through the wounds which Jesus carries. Jesus said: 'Peace be with you,' and immediately we are told 'he showed them his hands and his side'. This was all Thomas needed.

Greetings don't necessarily heal wounds or mend brokenness but genuine healing takes place after we admit, and deal with, our woundedness. Jesus was not ashamed of his wounds. Facing our woundedness is the first step to our redemption.

Neither is doubt an obstacle to salvation. Thomas was a proud doubter too. Honest doubt is both dignified and real.

So brokenness, failure and doubt are the human journey towards holiness, faith and hope. Jesus wasn't ashamed of his wounds, Thomas wasn't ashamed of his doubts. The gospel says it is possible to doubt and believe at the same time. One cannot be a disciple without being wounded. A preacher, teacher, politician, or anyone with power essentially sets out to change others. A disciple however is willing to be changed themselves. And that's the difference.

God loves each of us in times of faith and in times of doubt.

It is striking how often Jesus shared meals with friends and strangers alike. He knew the value of a meal, a chat and a bit of fun. He fed five thousand, he endured the Last Supper, he ate with Mary and Martha and dined with tax collectors. After the Resurrection he had breakfasts on the seashore and meals with those who invited him into their company.

Jesus makes himself known after his Resurrection not in a Temple, but rather at a meal with two friends he met along the road to Emmaus. In life we all have Emmaus moments. There are moments of doubt, confusion and disappointment. And we wonder where God is. The consolation comes when we realise that Jesus travels silently with us without imposition and without being noticed.

People often write to me to share their thoughts. This is part of a longer letter sent to me by a married woman with two adult children:

'I often heard you say that people have to take responsibility for their own decisions about faith. I have been lucky enough to attend some seminars with a group of parishes recently. What amazed me most was that the priest/minister/lay people who speak at these events have a completely different attitude to what is preached at Sunday Masses. Why can't the people who attend Sunday Mass hear the same enlightened material? The answer probably is that they are afraid the laity might start to think for themselves after years of being told what to do. It is so liberating to find that priests and laity are not so sure of anything anymore but still hang in there trying to work things out. That in itself is comforting.

'To me the message of Jesus is simple. Love God and love your neighbour. Life is about respecting the world and the people in it and treating everyone as equal. In the Acts of the Apostles we hear what the early church was like. It was simple, people lived in common, prayed with those who were sick and healed each other. They ate, they shared, they prayed and they grew.

'My problem is this. How in God's name did we get to the present era with clerics cut off from reality through their training, with structures that make it almost impossible to find a loving God anymore?'

George Bernard Shaw once said: 'Those who say it cannot be done, should not interrupt those who are already doing it.' We give too much heed to people who say 'it cannot be done'. There are people whose whole life is working to prove that 'it cannot be done' and being a proper nuisance to those who are already rolling up their sleeves and doing the impossible.

The early Christian community did not know they were founding a church. All they wanted was to try to live their lives as Jesus had told them to. Eventually they regained their strength and courage to preach the risen Jesus. They never preached a dead Jesus; they preached that Jesus *is* risen and lives among us. It was a message people wanted to hear and one which they reacted positively to. That in turn brought problems. They came to realise that there were poor people being neglected within the community. The preachers could not do everything. And so they were caught between two goods, the good of looking after the poor and the good of spreading the word that Jesus is risen – the good news of the gospel.

They hit on a plan. They were not trapped behind traditions. They recognised the Spirit was leading not only them but others too. So they asked for volunteers to look after the poor and had no trouble finding them. They prayed over them, anointed them, affirmed them in their ministry. Meanwhile they went on preaching the good news. That is how the Christian community grew. There was a welcome for every talent. There was no such thing as one gift being greater than another. All gifts are from God and all gifts were used for the spreading of God's kingdom.

Wouldn't it be wonderful if the church today could see that? Is there really any need for priests to be celibate old bachelors? Could there not be a new way of recognising God's many vocations among us?

There is a meaning to life. There is a purpose. There is a place of peace beyond this mess in which we now live.

Maya Angelou has been an inspiration to me through poetry and common sense. She died at the age of eighty-six after an eventful life. She had a tragic life in childhood, overcame it to become a stage actor and a dancer/entertainer. She became a world-famous author and towards the end of her life she was best known as a philosopher and poet. She is well known for inspirational common sense quotations, like this one, for example: 'You may not control the events that happen to you, but you can decide not to be reduced by them.'

Her wisdom was sought out by many people. One of her great themes in life was: 'If you don't like something, change it; if you can't change it, change your attitude.' She had an unshakeable faith in the goodness of human nature, but she also recognised that we have a great capacity to deceive ourselves. She once said: 'We are only as blind as we want to be.'

What has become known as the 'Tuam baby scandal' is truly horrifying, although it is only one of several similar stories. 796 babies and young children died in a Mother and Baby Home in Tuam. They were buried in a mass grave that was formerly a septic tank. We have no details about how they died; we will probably never know.

It is a frightening, awful, shocking thing. It happened in our own lifetime, not in the distant past. It happened when families said rosaries and ninety-seven per cent of the population went to Mass every week. It happened at a time when we were sending missionaries all over the world saving the lives of babies in 'pagan' countries.

Now we know that babies from a certain class in society were allowed to be hidden away in Mother and Baby Homes, in overcrowded and unhealthy conditions, where many of them died. Those who died were buried at night in a mass grave.

It was a tragic, awful time. It cannot be justified and all we can do is humbly ask God for forgiveness that such a thing could be done in his name and to ensure it never happens again.

Maybe the following simple prayer would be worth meditating upon: 'Send forth your Spirit, Lord, and renew the face of the earth.'

Music expresses depths of our emotional life that otherwise remain unspoken and perhaps are unspeakable. It makes sense of our feelings. And that's why St Hildegard wrote: 'God is music; God is life that nurtures every creature in its kind.'

God is music. God is love. God is everything that is good, expressing the inexpressible. Do not take the mystery out of God. Celebrate God as mystery. Celebrate God's unknowability. In the Old Testament we are told that the prophet Elijah was asked to stand on the mountain because the Lord was going to pass by. He sets out to look for and listen to God. A great wind comes that splits rocks and mountains but he concludes 'The Lord is not there.' Then there is an earthquake, but 'The Lord is not there.' After the earthquake, a fire, but 'The Lord is not there.'

Finally, there was 'a sound of sheer silence' and it is in the silence that God speaks to Elijah and directs him gently. God is not in the great and powerful shattering images. God is in the silence.

In Jesus, God speaks *our* language. We recognise that God is in our time and is not in a far distant place. God is part of our family, our community, our world, our history. In Jesus we see God, touch God, talk with God, listen to God and laugh with God. We experience God's compassion.

There once was a herd of elephants which the owners wanted to train to live in their own patch. A visitor noticed there was a thin little rope tied to the leg of each elephant which seemed to keep them in their territory.

It was obvious that if the elephant bothered to flick a leg it would break the rope. So the visitor was curious about this and asked the herdsman about it. The visitor was told that when the elephants were small a rope was tied around their leg. At that time it *was* strong enough to hold them within their territory. The elephants became so conditioned that they accepted the rope could contain them. When they grew up to be strong and big they still were constrained by a tiny rope. They simply did not break out of their conditioning.

Many of us are the same. We hang on to our beliefs and views and horizons because we have become conditioned to accept false limitations.

There is a principle in the spiritual life: 'Your image of God created you.' And if this is so, it is important to ask, and to go on asking, what kind of God do I believe in – what is my image of God?

Bad understandings of religion get in the way of a mature spiritual life. Religion should set us free; more often than not it entraps us in a set of customs, beliefs and practices which are little more than superstition. Spirituality creates willing people who can let go of their need to be first, their need to be right, their need to be saved, and, most of all, the need to feel superior to other people.

Mature believers let the Word of God change them rather than *using* the Word of God to change others.

We go on seeking Jesus no matter what happens us. Jesus did *not* say 'when you are healed from your sickness then you can begin to love'; he did not say 'when you are feeling loving then you can begin to love'. Nor did he say 'when you get what you want in life then you can begin to love.' It is not a matter of getting our lives together so that we can love. No. The commandment is to love now no matter what the circumstances of our life.

To be a Christian and follow Jesus is a way of life, not a way of worship. Jesus never said 'Worship me' but he did say 'Follow me.' That's why it's a way of life; it's a way of being in the world that is simple, shared, non-violent, peaceful and loving.

St Francis of Assisi wrote to his followers advising that they should be careful about how they pray. He said: 'When I pray I ask two questions. Who are you, God? Who am I?'

The spiritual life is finding out the God we believe in (who are you, God?), and then finding where I fit in (who am I?).

I listened to a programme on the radio once about silence, particularly long periods of silence which force us to have a conversation with ourselves and to look at issues within ourselves. Sometimes this confrontation with ourselves is more than we can handle. Zen Buddhism suggests that when we are in a period of silence and issues we cannot really face come to the surface, we simply:

> Let them come
> Let them be
> Let them go

What is usually known as the parable of the sower is also the parable of the seed. The sower plants in hope, but the quality of the ground on to which the seeds fall is critically important. Jesus preached the word and left it to germinate. He planted acts of kindness and tenderness, of goodness and healing, of mercy in places that, to the observer, might not produce growth. The religious leaders were often the rocky ground where Jesus' words did not find enough soil to grow. The outcasts and the lowly often proved the most fertile ground for the hope that Jesus gave.

The parable of the sower and the seed is an invitation to hope. We sow, God produces the harvest. How it happens is beyond knowing.

We have been accustomed, through churches and experience, to look for God only in spectacular events – in the mighty and in the miraculous. Jesus tells us that is not where we should look for God. God is in the small and in the insignificant bits and pieces of life. The parables teach us that life is more than what we see. Whilst we struggle through life, something mysterious is going on around us and within us. Whether we recognise it or not, God is at work in the world.

The prophet Ezekiel used the mighty cedar as a symbol of the assembly of God's people – big, imposing and majestic in appearance. Jesus, however, chose to use the image of the mustard seed for his vision of church – a tiny seed that grows into an unspectacular shrub with room for all that need shelter within.

Our church should be likewise. Not imposing, not mighty, not dominating all around it, but an unspectacular shrub at the side of the road, open and welcoming to all who need shelter.

In South Africa a medic was trying to keep a group of AIDS sufferers in a hospital engaged in life with some hope. One of her colleagues suggested that art might be a helpful way of encouraging them to express themselves.

Given the poverty in the township there were no canvases on which to work. But the medic got a bright idea. They put an appeal out for all the used teabags dumped around the township. They slit them open, emptied the tea leaves and placed the empty tea bags in a huge pot to boil them. They were then dried and glued to hardboard. When it was all done, the result was a usable 'canvas' for art.

One of the AIDS patients said: 'Isn't it amazing that we are able to make a masterpiece out of a mess?'

And that is a gospel principle and, indeed, what God does with us each day. Most of our lives are a mess because we fail to focus on what is important. God has a masterpiece ready to be made as soon as we co-operate, and it is truly wonderful to make a masterpiece out of a mess wherever it happens. Each of us is a treasure, a pearl of great price, a work of art.

To live a fruitful life we need to know what we're looking for.

A mother watched her son as he took part in a football match. He jumped to catch a ball but then suddenly dropped down to his knees on the grass. She thought he was injured but after a little while all the others gathered around him and searched for a few minutes for the contact lens that had dropped out of his eye. But of course the match was more important so they told him to go off and they'd play on anyway.

The mother had marked the spot and at half-time she went in, got down on her knees and after scrutinising the grass she found the contact lens. She brought it to her son who was truly amazed. 'How did you find the contact lens there?' he asked. She answered: 'We were looking for two different things. You were looking for a piece of plastic. I was looking for €200.'

A search can begin only after we realise that there is something valuable which is worth looking for. What is really valuable is often under our noses; we do not see it because we do not know its value. Nothing is more important than seeking God with a sincere heart. Everything else is superfluous and everything else can wait. That is important for people and it is also important for the church. What is the point in having a great edifice built if there is little real faith at its foundation? If there is a faith in the love and knowledge of God and his Son, Jesus Christ, and if that faith is real, we will not need laws to keep us on the straight and narrow.

The famous Jewish writer Elie Wiesel has written extensively about humanity's search for meaning. This arose from an extraordinary time in his life. Wiesel, together with his father, mother and sister were arrested in 1944 and taken in a cattle truck to Auschwitz concentration camp. At the gates of the camp the family were split in two – the father and son went to one camp, the mother and daughter to another. That was the last that Elie Wiesel ever saw of his mother and sister. He did see his father a couple of times again in the camp but then one day another prisoner told him that his father had died.

Elie Wiesel was alone but survived the ordeal of the extermination camp. Ever since he has written about what the extraordinarily cruel treatment of the camp did to human beings. In one of his books, *Night,* he recalls that he saw so many awful things there that he could no longer believe in God. In the camp he lost his family, he lost hope, he lost his innocence and he lost his faith. He has on many occasions said that the loss of faith was the worst thing that could have happened to him because with faith the rest might have been bearable.

Viktor Frankl, who also suffered in the Nazi concentration camps, said: 'Those who have a "why" to live, can bear with almost any "how".'

In the gospels Jesus is continually shown to be someone who believes in people above systems. Yet in the story of the Canaanite woman who comes to Jesus to plead for healing for her daughter, we hear what seems to be a harsh response by Jesus. He tells her that 'it is not fair to take the children's food and throw it to the dogs'. He tells her that his mission is to the people of Israel only.

As both a woman and a Gentile, the Canaanite woman was doubly marginalised in the Israelite society of the time, yet it did not stop this brave woman persisting in her attempt to convince Jesus to heal her daughter. The woman did not dispute Jesus' claim that his mission was to the Israelites, but made the observation that '… even the dogs eat the crumbs that fall from their master's table'. Her faith against what seemed like impossible odds, won Jesus' attention and ultimately, his respect.

Because Jesus agreed to heal the woman's daughter, despite the strict division between Jew and Gentile, he set an example for the Christian Church to do the same. Cultural barriers are just that – cultural. They have become so through practice over generations. That does not mean they have to remain forever more. Jesus has shown that cultural barriers are not a stumbling block to faith and healing. Jesus brought healing not just to the faithful but to *all* in need of healing.

Today we in the church give the heretical impression that only the perfect are worthy of being allowed into the presence of Jesus. Those in second relationships, as well as those struggling to remain in contact with the church whilst being true to their own sexuality (LGBT), and not forgetting those on the margins of belief, could do with at least a crumb of comfort.

Jesus was generous and did not believe in crumbs. There was always a welcome for the marginalised. It is time to open our hearts to all sincere, good, brave people represented by the Canaanite woman.

Rabbi Harold Kushner tells a wonderful story about a couple who were married for fifty-two years. The wife got Alzheimer's disease and was in the advanced stages of it, residing in a nursing home. Every day her loving husband went in with pictures of grandchildren, news about her neighbours, stories about what was happening in the neighbourhood and spoke to her as if she understood everything.

He knew, of course, she did not know who he was, never mind who he was talking about. Yet, every day he did it with great devotion. After spending a few hours chatting to him as if she was fully aware of what was going on, he would hold her hand, tell her he loved her, kiss her on the cheek and go home.

Kushner could not understand how anyone could do this. So Kushner asked him why he bothered going to see his wife every day when she didn't even know who he was. And the old man quietly replied: 'I go to see my wife because *I* know who *I* am.'

I think that we need to begin our journey of faith by pondering that wonderful question, 'Who am I?' It is only when I have wrestled with that question that I can possibly answer, 'Who do you say I am.'

Faith is about knowing who I am and then knowing who God is.

The actor Martin Sheen has often spoken about how his life fell apart during the filming of the very successful film, *Apocalypse Now*. He drank heavily, had no peace, was confused about who he was and why he was here. This led him into a period of despair. While still in his thirties, he had a near-fatal heart attack. While he was recovering, he realised that he could not separate his health problems from his spiritual ones.

Later, while making a film in Paris, he visited an English-speaking Catholic church on Avenue Hoche. And whilst praying there he recalled that he felt like, 'a new convert who returned home'. That was a defining moment in his life.

He knew that the church he grew up in was long gone and he had to re-enter a different church. 'I learned that I had to stand for something … that to keep my life from becoming self-contained and useless I had to feel other people's pain and act to help them. That is what faith and love are about …. Martin Luther King said that the church is a place to go forth from, not a place to escape reality.'

Keys have a dual purpose. They can lock a door to keep people out or they can open a door to let the whole world in. For too long the church has used keys in the former way – locking doors against people; keeping people out of God's kingdom. Telling them how sinful and how unworthy they are.

God's kingdom, however, is for everybody. God understands all the personal journeys we choose to make.

Jesus is looking for a personal commitment from each of us to keep on searching. Knowing in our head is not enough. Faith that does not change the way we live is not a real faith. Faith that is merely practice is not faith. When Jesus washes Peter's feet, we all have a foot in that basin.

I never met Br Roger Schutz. And I've never visited Taizé. But all my life I've read the works of Br Roger, who was stabbed to death in his own church in Taizé at the age of ninety in August 2005. The person who stabbed him was a mentally-ill woman and it is the ultimate irony that the man who lived a life of peace, reconciliation and forgiveness should be stabbed at prayer in a place he founded to bring people together sixty-five years ago.

Br Roger was the son of a Lutheran pastor and a French Protestant mother. In 1940 he visited the village of Taizé with the idea of founding a Protestant monastic community. But later he 'was astonished to see that Christians who while talking about the God of love, wasted so much energy justifying division'.

Initially he helped abandoned children and young Jews who were fleeing from Nazi persecution. He himself had to abandon Taizé in 1942 but returned in 1944 with a group of ecumenically-minded friends to set up a community. In Br Roger's words: 'I discovered my Christian identity by reconciling within myself my Protestant origins and my faith in the Catholic Church.'

He went on to spend his life building bridges, encouraging peace, helping reconciliation and preaching forgiveness. Not only did he help Jews but he also welcomed groups from Northern Ireland, Rwanda, Bosnia and every troubled spot in the world.

As Taizé grew to be a centre of prayer and peace for Europe, developers saw its potential and wanted to turn it into another Lourdes. He told the developers he couldn't stop them building hotels, but if they did he promised to move his monastery elsewhere.

Much of Schutz's writing was idealistic and frequently conservative. But I have on my desk a quote, which has guided me for many years now. He said: 'However powerless we may be, God calls us to bring reconciliation where there are oppositions, and hope where there is anxiety. God calls us to make his compassion for human beings accessible by the way we live.'

During the Special Olympics opening ceremony held in Croke Park in June 2003, one Olympian down on the field had his camera pointed directly at the very spot where the celebrities were in the Hogan Stand. A professional photographer passed him by and noticed that his camera was pointing in the wrong direction. If he had taken a photograph it would have been a perfect photograph of his eye.

The photographer gently told him that he would get a much better photograph if he turned the camera the other way. Instantly the young man looked at him and said: 'Thanks, but I've discovered that if I look into it this way I can get a closer view of them.' The photographer took his lesson, went off and knew that the aim for every photographer is to have a different angle.

A lot depends on our ability to look at life differently.

Suffering and crosses are not of value in themselves but once we decide to follow God, obstacles will be part of the journey. Discipleship will involve suffering, often unjustly. Nothing in life is simple and nothing in life comes easy. Jesus' command in the gospel to anyone who wanted to follow him was to be prepared to deny themselves and take up their cross and follow him. This was not an invitation to seek out suffering for its own sake. It is not a way of life to be chosen for itself. Rather it is preparation for the likely rejection, ridicule and suffering that goes with trying to be a Christian disciple and being a prophetic voice.

A prophet is 'someone whose utterances become the consciences of the people. A prophet is someone who warns people of the future consequences of their present actions'. (Dr Martin Luther King Jnr)

Nobody can be judged by the worst acts of their life. Neither can we be judged solely by our best acts. None of us is as bad as our worst selves and none of us is as perfect as our best selves. The truth is somewhere in between. Ultimately, only God will judge.

St Paul told us that the message of the cross is foolishness to those who do not understand it, but for those who do, it is the power of God.

Elber Twomey lost her husband, Con, her son, Oisin, and her unborn baby daughter, Elber Marie, and she herself was badly injured, when a suicidal man deliberately swerved across a busy dual carriageway and crashed head-on into their car. In a radio interview on RTÉ, Elber spoke of waking up after the crash and finding a priest by her hospital bed.

Faith is important to her family but she admitted that she was resentful, bitter and anxious having to face life without her loved ones. The priest suggested that if she could pray for the man who killed her family, she might begin to move on from his terrible influence on her life. She told the priest he would be a very old man if he waited for that to happen.

Yet three months later she found herself beginning to pray for the driver and she began to experience the healing the priest promised. She now prays to understand better what caused him to act as he did. Elber will never forget what happened to her and her family, but she can forgive the evilness of the act. In taking up her cross and following Jesus, her cross transformed from sheer evil into something life-giving.

In the parable of the labourers in the vineyard, Jesus likens the vineyard to the kingdom of heaven. Those who were hired at first light agreed to work for the standard day's wages for the job. As the day went on, more labourers were hired at mid-morning, mid-day, and still more mid-afternoon. When it was almost time to finish, the last workers were hired. Even though they agreed a fair day's wages, those who were hired at first light expected to be paid more than those hired later. The owner of the vineyard said: 'Am I not allowed to do what I choose with what belongs to me? Or are you envious because I am generous?'

Sometimes, we do not understand and, therefore, cannot tolerate God's generosity to others. We expect an easy judgement for ourselves, but resent God's generosity to others. Luckily, God does not give to any of us what we deserve. All is grace.

The Christian community is the presence of God lived visibly among God's people: 'Where two or three people are gathered in my name, I shall be among them.' True renewal in the church starts with the believing community, not monstrous organisations. It starts with each individual within that believing community, who asks: How can I …

- Speak the truth in charity and in a way that inspires others to live in truth and love?
- Help create a loving, prayerful, helpful gathering called the Christian community?
- Make God's love real in the world in which we live?
- Be a good Samaritan church, showing practical compassion, to do good works and not just *talk* about them?
- Bring about a more open, welcoming community and church in my area?
- Be a church which helps all of us to be better, more rounded people?

This is a challenge, but not an overwhelming one. Each of us has a gift to bring. We cannot be the hurler on the ditch. If we do not do and encourage what is right, then we are complicit in the wrong that takes place because of our silence.

The Jewish writer Isaac Asimov once said in an interview: 'If my doctor told me I had only six minutes to live, I wouldn't brood, I would type faster.' We should live until the moment we die. Many of us have stopped living, and are just waiting to be buried.

The sculptor Timothy Schmalz was returning to his parents' home in Toronto for Christmas. The weather was freezing cold and Schmalz noticed a homeless person wrapped in blankets on a park bench. The stark contrast between the life of this homeless man and the welcome he was assured of receiving from his parents had a deep effect on Schmalz. He told his parents that he had just seen Jesus lying on a park bench. He took this as his inspiration and started a new sculpture.

First of all he sculpted an extra long bench. Then he cast a bronze of a man lying the full length of the bench. From his memory he had a striking image of the homeless man pulling the blanket over his head so that nobody would recognise him. But because he pulled the blanket over his head, his feet became exposed.

At first our eyes are drawn to the head of the man covered with the blanket and then we begin to notice his feet. And as you look at his feet you notice the stigmata or the wounds of Christ on both his feet. Schmalz called his sculpture *The Homeless Jesus*.

There is an additional twist to the story. Two major Catholic cathedrals turned down the opportunity to have the first cast – St Michael's in Toronto and then St Patrick's in New York, both citing renovations as the reason. The Jesuit school of theology at the University of Toronto, Regis College, now houses the first cast of this deeply moving sculpture. Since it was first put on display, a number of casts of the statue have now been erected in several cities. The first sculpture to be sold outside of North America was to Ireland and has been given space in the grounds of Christ Church Cathedral, Dublin.

The statue is provocative, and this is precisely what the sculptor intended. When it was initially put on display, some people were very uncomfortable with the image of Jesus it portrayed. It upset their comfortable image of God. Jesus was anything but comfortable, as we know from the gospels, and one of the greatest challenges is in the Gospel of Matthew that inspired Schmalz: 'Truly, I tell you, just as you did it to one of the least of these who are members of my family, you did it to me.'

Jesus teaches us by the conduct of his everyday life. He goes to the most despised and discriminated against. He eats with sinners. He allows the rejects of the world to kiss his feet. He touches lepers and lives with the risk. He is friends with sinners. He seeks out the lost so that he can save them.

The people we turn away from, God comes closest to. The people we humiliate, God defends. The people we push away, Jesus accepts as his best friends. Jesus tells us the people we reject have a privileged place in God's plan. The leaders, who are causing so much trouble for Jesus, preach their version of God but in the process drive people away from the true God. They make people's lives harder than they need be, and for Jesus that is almost an unforgivable sin.

Richard Rohr says that sin can sometimes teach us more than virtue can. Conversion is when we learn from the wrong we do; when we recognise that all sin has consequences for ourselves and others.

I once spoke to a man whose great hobby was building dry stone walls. Naturally enough I was interested as to how he could cut the stones to fit so perfectly. And he surprised me by saying that he tries his best never to cut stones. He never rejects a stone either. He takes each stone, finds a place for it in the wall and then builds around it, even if there are spaces left in the wall.

If you start looking for the perfect stone you will never build a wall. Take each stone as they come and find room for them and the wall will build itself. It is inspiring to know that there is always a space found for each stone no matter what its shape or size. He said: 'It's not a jigsaw I'm putting together, where everything has to fit perfectly. The gaps and the spaces in the wall allow the wind to blow through and so strengthen the wall.'

I regularly consult a spiritual director. In my early years there was one I did not get on with all that well. He was not much impressed with me either. We were not there to be friends, but for me to get some focus in my spiritual life. I asked him a difficult question: What must I do to please God?

He answered with a bit of a puzzle. He said:

> Abraham accepted strangers – God was pleased.
> Elisha did not accept the stranger – God was pleased.
> David was proud – God was pleased.
> The publican was ashamed – God was pleased.
> John the Baptist lived in a desert – God was pleased.
> Jonah rushed off to the city – God was pleased.

I learned that if you walk the road of integrity, the world will be a better place, and God will be pleased.

In his time Jesus would have been seen as a reformer in the Jewish faith, not someone who started a new religion. Those deeply observant of the letter of the law, the Pharisees, were concerned about this reform-mindedness. To test Jesus one of them asked which of all the 613 laws of Judaism were the most important to keep. Of the 613 laws, 248 were positive commands as in 'You shall …' and 365 were negative as in 'You shall not …'

Jesus answered with part of a Jewish prayer that was recited every morning by every good Jew (which really meant every male Jew). It is a biblical prayer and is known as the *Shema*: 'You shall love the Lord your God with all your heart, and with all your soul and with all your might.'

Jesus tells us that this is the first and greatest commandment, and there is a second one like it: 'You shall love your neighbour as yourself. On these two commandments hang all the law and the prophets.' In other words, all the laws of religion are built on the foundation of these two commandments. Without those foundations, everything else falls. We cannot love God and ignore suffering.

Without love everything else is futile. So it is not enough for me to ask myself: 'Do I believe in, or do I love, God?' The question is: 'Do I love my suffering neighbour?' Do I support or challenge the structures that imprison people in their suffering, whether those structures are societal, religious, political or from whatever source?

There is a kind of thought pattern going around now that we should not use the word 'death'. People 'pass on' or even 'have passed'. I know it is well intentioned, but really it is a denial of the death process. As people of faith we are not to be afraid of death. There is no other way to get to heaven. We have to die and, for a Christian, death brings new life. Those who have left here are in a new place, have not forgotten us and we are still connected to them.

Alfred Nobel invented and mass-produced explosives, including dynamite, and became extremely wealthy in the process. When his brother Ludwig (also a very wealthy and successful industrialist) died, the press mistakenly thought it was Alfred and published his obituary.

Alfred Nobel was horrified to read that, among other unflattering comments, he was being remembered as 'a man who made it possible to kill more people more quickly than anyone else who ever lived'.

He took stock of his life and set up the Nobel Peace Prize and also the Nobel Prizes for literature, the sciences, medicine and economics to encourage positive work for humanity. He said in later life that 'every person ought to have the chance to correct their epitaph in mid-life and to write a new one.'

As well as remembering our faithful departed, it is to ask ourselves how faithful are we, and how will we be remembered when we become part of the community of the departed. What kind of epitaph are you and I writing now?

A favourite poet of mine, Francis Ledwidge from Slane in Co. Meath, initially opposed Irish men fighting for the British Army. However, he was persuaded by John Redmond that Home Rule could be granted if the Irish fought in the Great War, so he joined the army himself. He was killed in July 1917. From the front, on the night before his departure, he wrote these words:

> And now I'm drinking wine in France
> The helpless child of circumstance
> Tomorrow will be loud with war
> How will I be accounted for?

And that is the challenging thought: 'How will I be accounted for?' Causes, institutions, buildings, churches and canon laws are essentially about power. We should be careful what we commit our lives to. How will I be accounted for? This is the great question.

Boris Pasternak once said: 'When great moments knock on the door of your life, they knock no louder than the beat of your heart … and it is easily missed.' Treasure the miraculous that is there in the ordinary.

God does not need buildings to dwell in but we need places to be together as a community. Those who are locked into authority will tell you of the importance of parishes and boundaries. Jesus highlighted the importance of communities living, praying and being together, helping each other. Those communities come together round the table of the Lord and are not affected by lines on maps. It is the praying community that counts. People are more important than boundaries and, indeed, people are more important than buildings. We have to learn first, as believing communities, to recognise God in the faces of all who stumble along the path of life.

There are many ways of experiencing community. New Horizons is one such community. It was set up by Action Mental Health in Northern Ireland to help people overcome the effects of mental ill-health and to facilitate a return to work. Members find practical and emotional support through a variety of means. There is a well-equipped gym, art and craft classes, computer classes, back-to-work courses and mental health courses. There are a range of expert tutors and counsellors who help those seeking to overcome abuse of alcohol and drugs. It is a community caring for those who need to be cared for. It is everything our church should and could be.

On 17 November 2014 the funeral took place of the Jesuit priest, Gerard Hughes. He did not escape the notice of the church authorities after he publicly stated he could not accept the birth control encyclical *Humanae Vitae*, and was twice dismissed from appointments.

When he was about fifty years old, Fr Gerard recognised that he was suffering greatly from depression. He became, in his own words, 'a confused, bewildered and disillusioned Christian'. He decided to walk on a pilgrimage to Rome, thinking, reflecting and wondering and coming to terms with his own life and his own journey.

Out of that pilgrimage came the book *God of Surprises*. In it he dismantled the various images of God which destroy all our lives. For example, he has a famous description of God as Uncle George – a lovely, old uncle who lives in a mansion far away but who has plenty of bribes to dispense to those who please him. However, down in the basement there was a massive furnace for those who did not agree to be controlled by him.

And so Hughes went through God images, one being a Policeman God who is always catching us out and wanting to arrest us and put us in prison, checking out if we have broken any little law.

This was the part of the book which, when I read it, empowered me to reject all these false gods that not only the church believed in, but I often preached.

He went on to reveal a God that we could believe in. A God for the lost, for those who cannot forgive themselves, for the stumblers and the agnostics who hardly dare to believe that God is within them. We become content to know that God is a mystery that we'll never understand fully but who frees us. God is greater than any church or any person and it is not possible for the conscious mind to grasp God.

Gerard Hughes freed me and others to begin to look at the real God of love and not the tyrannical, false God of religion.

According to Hughes the basic question we should dwell on is: 'What do I long for more than anything else in the whole world?'

Get in touch with a God that makes you realise that you're much greater than you thought. This was the God that kept Fr Gerard Hughes going during bouts of depression and gave him hope to give us hope.

The gospel story of the talents is well known. In this case the talent is not a natural gift or skill. In biblical times a talent was a unit of currency based on a given weight of a precious metal such as gold or silver. The slaves in the story were entrusted with something of high value and the risks were great if they invested badly or lost the money. So there was much at stake.

Two of the three slaves doubled the value of the talents they had received, but the third slave was frightened of the risk and the predictable wrath of his master if he did not do well, so he buried his talent. He played safe and lost everything. He was thinking only of himself and his own security and so would not risk making a mistake.

As with all parables, there is a message here. The gospel is urging us to say 'no' to our obsession with security. And to say 'yes' to the God who encourages us to risk, to change the world and to spend the gifts that we have for our faith.

It is the only way to use the gift of faith. He's saying 'no' to a faith that's buried in conformity and 'yes' to committing ourselves to following Jesus even though we don't know where we will be led. The only security we need is God's promise.

I am not easily shocked but one interview on RTÉ radio left me stunned. A fireman was talking about being called out to an accident (I cannot remember exactly where) in which a two-and-half-year-old child was killed. He was horrified that so many people stopped to take a picture of the child lying on the road. Worse still, the size of the crowd meant that his men could hardly get in to help the child.

He thought it was a new low in Irish society and I agree, wholeheartedly. Another fireman phoned in with his experience of this disturbing trend. A man was on top of a bridge threatening to throw himself into the river Liffey. A crowd of passersby gathered around him and rather than helping him to come down, they were taking his picture and putting it up on Facebook whilst waiting on him to jump.

When the fire brigade arrived, one idiot shouted out: 'Jump soon because I'm on my lunch hour.'

What kind of a society are we becoming?

We do not need to wait for our final judgement to judge our lives. It is happening now and we are setting up our judgement by the kind of lives we lead. What measures our destiny is not the religion we belong to; rather it is the compassion we show and the justice we work for. What pleases God is to help those who need ministering to.

No religion is pleasing to God unless it inspires its people to compassion for the last, the lost and the least.

It is not enough to say 'I never do much wrong,' as many of us do when we come to confession. That is the ultimate admission of a lack of self-knowledge.

First of all none of us should be complimented because we have not done much wrong. That is the very least we are called to. If you have not done much wrong have you specifically done anything good? Have I done any good? What do I do to help? Whom do I help? How am I working for justice?

It is not enough to give money although it is a start. Giving money to the poor is worse than useless if that money has been obtained unjustly. If it has then it is not a charity to give it to the poor, it's a duty to give it away because it is not ours in the first place.

Finally, we are asked to feed the hungry as a start. After that we have to work to change the system which caused the hunger.

Waiting is not part of our modern culture. Everything is instant. It is probably true to say that we have forgotten how to wait. We expect instant solutions to our problems, like water from a tap. We have perpetual links to the Internet and we are never disconnected. But, as I was once reminded, constant access to knowledge is no substitute for wisdom.

Life is not a disjointed journey but is a pilgrimage. We are not on a journey to God; God *is* the journey and God *is* the destination. We have to recognise the signs and promptings of God in our lives, particularly in the day-to-day events of life.

There are no right answers to wrong questions. We have to begin by valuing the question more than the answer. The questions peel off our attitudes and help us to be more open to God's leadership within us. I have to keep asking honest questions without desiring the right answers. Sadly, many of us have set answers/prejudices in life and we ask only questions which lead to those answers. To call that by its proper name, it is personal delusion.

The Christian journey according to gospel spirituality is always about 'the More'. Think of the rich young man story in the gospel. He led a perfect life. He did everything right. He kept the commandments. He attended his religious duties. He felt contented with his life. But deep down he knew he had to ask a further question.

So he met Jesus and he asked him that question. It is a question we should ask ourselves on a daily basis too. And the question is: 'What should I do to inherit eternal life?'

The answer Jesus gave was simple: 'Sell everything you have, give it to the poor and come follow me.' That was the More Jesus wanted him to reach for. But he was not ready for that journey to the More.

The gospel tells us that he turned and walked away and he was sad. It's interesting that *he* was sad but it doesn't say Jesus was sad. Jesus did not run after him; he allowed him to make his own choices. We have no idea what happened later in life or whether he ever did accept that invitation to leave behind the security of his religious practices and to throw himself on the mercy of God. But that was the More that was revealed to him by the right question. The answer was one that he could not agree with or choose at this time. So it meant he was going to have to ask himself a lot more questions to get to that point.

Who is my neighbour?

Jesus told the parable of the Good Samaritan to answer this question. The religious people were so intent on being religious that they forgot how to be helpful. They forgot that they had a neighbour. They were so concerned with ritual that humans in need didn't enter their life story.

So, Jesus then told them about a man who would have been considered an outcast in Jewish culture. He was a Samaritan. His goodness was shown by the fact that he took care of the man, paid for his accommodation and care, and promised to come back and look after him again. Jesus asked a delightful question: 'Which of them do you think was a neighbour to that man?'

They answered the one who looked after him and Jesus gave them an answer they didn't expect: 'Go and do the same yourselves.' Point made!

So questions peel away our prejudices and trick us into launching out in a different direction. Sometimes it is a direction we would rather not take, but it is where we must go.

Repentance is not just a one-day event. Repentance means a commitment to change our ways. It is an acknowledgement of our own sinfulness. It is a time to go into the desert and look at life and listen to God's voice. It is a long period of soul-searching. Repentance is not making ourselves guilty for a while and moving on. Repentance means that we promise to look at things in a different way now. It will bring us a new outlook, new values and a change of heart. But it is not only about peripheral change. It is about transformation of our lives, our culture and our attitude to God and to others. That is what we are asked to by living our faith.

In each of our lives there is both darkness and light. In each of our lives we have to come to terms with both the good and the bad, the bright and the dark, the acceptable and the difficult to accept. Martin Luther King summed this idea up succinctly: 'Darkness cannot drive out darkness; only light can do that. Hate cannot drive out hate; only love can do that.' We can be so content to sit with our darkness that we never notice the light when it is offered to us. But if we are to overcome darkness, in our family, in our community, in our personal lives, then we have to welcome light and love into our lives.

The problem is that we get so used to living in the dark that we cannot come out into the light. St Paul had made that point often in his letters. 'People', he said, 'would rather live in darkness, than welcome the light of Christ into their lives.' He could have been talking about me!

A quotation which has been falsely attributed to Plato is useful nevertheless:

'We can easily forgive a child for being afraid of the darkness – but the real tragedy of life is when men [adults] are afraid of the light.'

As Christians the challenge for us is how do we let the light of Christ shine through us? Maturity means that we should never be afraid of sharing our lives with others, of overcoming secrecy, of refusing to live in our own selfish little worlds.

An outstanding light in dark places is the life of a young teenage girl, Malala Yousafzai. Born in Pakistan in 1997, by eleven years of age she was fighting for the right for girls to be educated. In 2012, while still campaigning, she was shot by a Taliban gunman, but thankfully survived. She was brought to England where her story went global. She rightly was honoured with the Nobel Peace Prize in 2014. In her acceptance speech, Malala asked:

'The world can no longer accept that basic education is enough. Why do leaders accept that for children in developing countries, only basic literacy is sufficient, when their own children do homework in Algebra, Mathematics, Science and Physics? ...

'Dear sisters and brothers, the so-called world of adults may understand it, but we children don't. Why is it that countries which we call "strong" are so powerful in creating wars but are so weak in bringing peace? Why is it that giving guns is so easy but giving books is so hard? Why is it, why is it that making tanks is so easy, but building schools is so hard?'

Nobody is perfect. We do not have to be perfect. Just be the best we can be. Accept that no matter how hard you try there will always be room for improvement. Do not look for perfection in yourself and do not look for perfection in others. Live like human beings because Jesus was quite happy to be a human being dealing with faults and failings.

Learn, with the help of others, to manage your problems. Work at things in your life so that your problems and imperfections do not define you. This happens when you manage them rather than letting them manage and define you.

Be aware how much other people try to manipulate you. Do not allow the dysfunction of others to control you.

I have spent most of my life as a leader in various Passionist communities. The most disturbing problems I have had to deal with were members of the community who, through their dysfunctional behaviour, wrecked the peace of community life.

Look around your own family; is there anybody there whom everybody dances around? Is there anybody who uses guilt as a means of control? Is there anybody in your workplace whom everybody tries to humour? Recognise that for what it is – manipulation.

Do not let the dysfunction of others rule your life. It is said that no people can steal my unhappiness unless I allow them to. There is a great deal of truth in that. Have enough freedom to be satisfied with what you are – less than perfect. Make the best of what you have, be willing to grow and be the best you can be.

Sometimes we assume the 'holy family' is some sort of model family for the rest of us. I do not think that is true. The holy family is a reminder to us that there are occasions when bad things happen to good people. A holy family is not the one which never has to cope with trouble, failures and weaknesses. The holy family accepts trouble, failure and weaknesses and finds God in them.

Every generation has to learn to be a family and to re-learn how to be parents anew in the changing world we live in. The family needs to have:

A sense of humour

A sense of gratitude

A sense of belonging.

We need a sense of humour to laugh at ourselves and to laugh at the ridiculous situations we get disturbed about.

We need a sense of gratitude because without gratitude we cannot be generous. We need to be aware of the many gifts we have been given, rather than to complain about what we haven't received.

We need a sense of belonging. I remember working with a group of homeless people, when I was asked the question: 'What do you think is the worst thing about being homeless?' I suggested things like not having a roof over your head, not having a bed, not having food, etc. They said all of those things were tough but believe it or not you can get used to them.

They then said the worst thing about being homeless was knowing that when you die no one will miss you. That really is a very powerful way of saying that we need to belong somewhere.

I will never forget what the Dominican philosopher Fr Herbert McCabe said in one of his lectures that I attended. I was not sure what it meant at the time but the older I get the more convinced I am of its truth. He said: 'We are not just human *beings*, we are human *becomings*.'

The single mystery of the Resurrection and Ascension and Pentecost makes us remember the resurrection of victory over death, the exultation of Jesus at the Ascension and the gift of the spirit at Pentecost.

Now that the Word of God is returned to God we become the compassion of Christ. St Teresa of Avila said: 'Christ has no body but yours on earth, no hands but yours on earth. No feet but yours on earth. Yours are the eyes he uses to look with compassion on the world; yours are the hands that bless the world.'

Each of us is a work of art; a canvas coloured carefully by God as he writes straight on the crooked lines of my life. We are all imperfect enough to be beautiful and loved exactly as we are.

There is good news to tell and the gospel says: 'Go to the whole world and spread the good news.' St Paul reminds us beautifully: 'Live a life worthy of the calling you have received. Be grateful, be holy, be yourself.'

When presiding at a baptism I point out two things.

Firstly, I ask each person there to recognise that the child is the only one who doesn't have to make a promise. The family and the community are making a promise to pass on their faith and their image of God to the innocent child who has been given to them by God. It is a good way to begin: are they promising to hand on a sense of faith, a sense of order in the chaos of life to the innocent child? Are they intending to give the child a chance to know God?

Secondly, I make this point. The blessing at the end of baptism says: 'May this child be helped by all of us who profess the same faith, to think of others in life, to work for others, and to be a good neighbour.' Nothing less than a mission statement for a Christian family.

The story of the Resurrection in the Gospel of Mark very strongly proclaims the good news that Jesus is raised by God. But it goes further and shows us the means we must take to see, to recognise and to meet the risen Jesus.

We shouldn't decide to remain living among the dead. Jesus is not to be found in the world of the dead.

To see Jesus we must go to Galilee. In other words we must retrace the steps of Jesus and see how he lived his life. Faithful following of Jesus is essential if we are to experience the resurrection in our own lives.

The Resurrection tells us that suffering and death will never have the last word. God will always be a God of surprises and new life. Nothing is impossible for God.

Dr Jeff Piehler, an American scientist, was diagnosed with incurable prostate cancer. (I know the feeling of a cancer diagnosis!) He upset his family though when he decided that he would build his own coffin. He thought it would be a celebration not only of life, but of his death as well. So he contacted an artist/carpenter whom he knew and they both designed and made the coffin. He said they made a beautiful pine box but also a beautiful lasting friendship whilst they were doing it.

Furthermore it taught him many lessons. He said: 'It's very hard to be angry at a slow driver in front of you when you've just come from sanding your own coffin.'

Material things take on a different aspect. There is not much room for grudges when you are measuring yourself for the coffin. You tend to see the goodness in others when you see it from that perspective.

You want to live every day to its full potential. And he ended by saying that his favourite line of poetry now was: 'I have loved the stars too fondly to be fearful of the night.'

Benjamin Franklin said: 'Remember not only to say the right thing in the right place, but far more difficult still, to leave unsaid the wrong thing at the tempting moment.'

Throughout his time as archbishop, Oscar Romero said over and over that, as church, we are called to cry out for justice when our leaders and authorities go astray. In a homily in April 1978 he preached: 'A church that doesn't provoke any crises, a gospel that doesn't unsettle, a word of God that doesn't get under anyone's skin, a word of God that doesn't touch the real sin of the society in which it is being proclaimed – what gospel is that?'

Seven Alternative Deadly Sins

1. I don't think

2. I don't know

3. I don't care

4. I'm too busy

5. I leave well enough alone

6. I have no time to read and find out

7. I am not interested

Mother Teresa was asked why she 'did not give a rod with which to fish, into the hands of the poor, rather than the fish itself, as this makes them remain poor.' Her response was: 'The people whom we pick up are not able to stand with a rod. So today I will give them fish and when they are able to stand, then I shall send them to you and you can give them the rod.'

Look and Listen

Moses said he was 'slow of speech',
Jeremiah said he was 'too young',
Amos said, 'I am no prophet',
Mary said, 'How can this be?'
Peter said he was 'too sinful',
The centurion said he was 'not worthy',
Paul said, 'I know that nothing good lives in me.'

Today it is your turn. God calls and doesn't ask if we are suitable – only if we are available.

Author unknown

Oscar Romero was archbishop for just three years. Initially he was a pious, conservative, run-of-the-mill cleric but he changed utterly when his friend Fr Rutilio Grande was murdered because of his work with the poor. Even though it was out of character, Romero took up the challenge and preached passionately against the unjust regime which impoverished the citizens.

'The church cannot absent itself from this struggle for liberation,' he said, 'but its presence in this trouble must lift up and respect human dignity ... I believe in the church that is a sign of the presence of God's love in the world where men and women extend their hands and encounter one another as sisters and brothers.'

When he preached the Sunday after the murder, he wanted no retaliation for Fr Grande's death: 'My brothers and sisters there should be no feeling of vengeance among us. We are concerned about the things of God who commands us to love him above all things and to love one another as we love ourselves ... there can be no true peace that is based on injustice or violence or intrigue.' He concluded with a powerful act of faith: 'We are a pilgrim church, exposed to misunderstanding and persecution, but we are a church that walks calmly because we carry within us the power of love.'

Take charge of your life. No one will make things happen for you. You have to make things happen for yourself. And no matter what bad things happen to you in life, do your best to turn it around. Use it to your advantage. The more you believe you have been dealt a bad hand, the more likely you are to crumble under failure. Just because you made a mistake, does not mean your life is a failure. Good people make mistakes. Good parents rear wayward children, good workers often lose jobs. Be positive. Positive people always take risks even when they are scared.

Break down your protective walls. More and more people, who are afraid of getting hurt, build walls around themselves. They trust no one. They keep people out of their lives at all costs. If you suddenly realise that all of your relationships are skin deep, you are in trouble. If you keep people out, they will never hurt you, but you'll never have a meaningful life either.

Be grateful. Those who are grateful for their gifts find it easier to be more positive than those who complain about gifts they do not have. Take time to reflect on what you have and be grateful for it.

Like yourself! It seems obvious when you say it – if you do not like yourself why should anybody else like you? If there are things about yourself that you do not like – change them. Do not use them as an excuse to hate yourself.

'When we have come to believe in the voices that call us worthless and unlovable, then success, popularity, and power are easily perceived as attractive solutions. The real trap, however, is self-rejection. As soon as someone accuses me or criticises me, as soon as I am rejected, left alone, or abandoned, I find myself thinking, "Well, that proves once again that I am a nobody." … [My dark side says,] I am no good … I deserve to be pushed aside, forgotten, rejected, and abandoned. Self-rejection is the greatest enemy of the spiritual life …' (Henri J. M. Nouwen)

In August 2014 a disturbing video entitled 'A message to America' appeared on the Internet. The freelance journalist James Foley was kneeling in front of the camera. With him was an executioner, entirely in black, who identified himself as a member of the Islamic State just before he decapitated the prisoner.

Thousands of miles away in Rochester, New Hampshire John and Diane Foley were being comforted by their pastor, Fr Paul Gousse. Remembering the incident the priest was himself inspired by how Foley's mother, Diane, accepted the terrible news. She asked the priest to pray for her and her family that they would never become bitter. That day the family issued a statement highlighting how their son James 'gave his life trying to expose to the world the suffering of the Syrian people. We implore the kidnappers to spare the lives of the remaining hostages and we thank Jim for all the joy he gave us. He was an extraordinary son, brother, journalist and person.'

Those who worked with him recognised two absolutes in his life – his family and his faith. John and Diane Foley taught their children to care for others and to work for justice. James Foley attended Marquette College, a Jesuit school in Milwaukee, famous for its dedication to social justice. When he graduated from Marquette College in 1996 he went on to teach voluntarily for a non-profit organisation with a mission to 'build the movement to eliminate educational inequity'.

Years later Foley changed focus to journalism. He graduated from the School of Journalism in 2008 and went on to teach English to the inmates in Cook County Jail in Chicago. In 2011 James Foley, together with American journalist Clare Morgana Gillis, a Spanish photographer, Manu Brabo, and a South African photo journalist, Anton Hammerl, were detained by Gaddafi supporters in Libya. Hammerl was shot and the other three were captured. Foley was held for forty-four days and Gillis later recalled that in captivity she began to realise how important faith was to Foley. She recalls his prayer was: 'Give us the strength to endure what this day brings; Give us the wisdom to face our captors; strengthen our families.'

Foley was a focused young man who 'never said an angry word to anyone, even to those who were holding him captive,' Gillis remembers. They were released without explanation in May 2011. Foley wrote: 'I began to pray the rosary whilst in captivity. It was what my mother and grandmother would have prayed. I said ten Hail Marys between each Our Father. It took a long time, almost an hour, to count one hundred Hail Marys on my knuckles. It helped to keep my mind focused.'

When he returned home his family, naturally, wanted him to find less dangerous employment in journalism. His local priest tried to convince him not to go back to the area where he had been captured. But Foley told the priest: 'Father I need to go back because the world needs to know the plight of people who are being walked on …' It was that decision which led to his capture and cruel decapitation last August in Syria.

There are always dedicated, heroic, faith-filled young people who risk everything, including life itself, in the cause of justice.

Jordan Spieth, the American professional golfer and 2015 Masters champion, set course records in Augusta and became the second youngest player ever to wear the iconic Green Blazer. However, for Jordan Spieth family has always come first, especially his younger sister Ellie who is autistic. His former athletic director at the Jesuit College Preparatory School in Dallas, Steve Koch said: 'Jordan is a genuine guy. He says what he believes. He believes in supporting others, taking care of others before he takes care of himself.'

The President of the Jesuit School, Michael Earsing, believes that the foundations of family, a balanced life, and caring for others, are values which will serve him well in the years ahead.

The Jesuit College believes that he will continue to be a role model for their pupils and all young people. 'I think', Earsing said, 'it's a hope of everyone who works in education that you see somebody who is achieving at such a high level, and who's also a wonderful model for students. Jordan is just the common man who achieved greatness with the blessings and talents God has given him.'

In her book *Hope Will Find You*, Naomi Levy tells of the wisdom she has learned from her daughter Noa, who struggles with a debilitating degenerative disease.

One morning in early September, little Noa woke up with a terrible bout of ataxia, the inability to keep her balance. Noa was teetering like someone who was severely drunk. Her mother wanted to keep her home from school, but Noa, just in her second week in second grade, would not hear of it. Noa told her mother: 'If I pray for a while, I'll be okay.' So Noa picked herself up, held on to the wall, made her way to her room, stood before the mirror, and started singing her morning prayers in Hebrew.

Her mother Naomi remembers: 'She sang with great joy and purity. I was watching from a distance, not wanting to disturb her or make her self-conscious. A serenity started to flow through her body. I could see it. Her mood changed, her posture changed, her expression changed. When she was done singing, she walked straight up to me with strength and steadiness and said, "I'm ready for school now." And she was. Prayer could do that for her.'

A hospital chaplain recounts a scene she has seen many times in her ministry: 'When a family gathers around a deceased loved one, the hospital bed becomes a sort of communion table. Around the bed there may be a weeping daughter, an ex-husband, a current partner, two sons who haven't spoken in years, an estranged sister, and a doting brother. When I enter the room, I instantly feel that I am in a sacred space. We form a circle and we pray. I say something as simple as: "Tell me about her," and the stories begin to flow, followed by laughter and tears. Held by love, people suspend their judgments and hurt feelings, if just for a moment. Such moments can be the beginning of a deeper kind of healing.' (Adapted from *Connections*)

A wise priest whom I respected greatly, who lived to be ninety-four, often said: 'It's no fun growing old.' As I now grow old myself, I can't argue with him.

But age has its compensations. It's easier to be yourself without having to put on a show. You don't need to protect yourself, your roles, or your status. You don't need to promote them, or prove them to anyone. You don't think of yourself as being superior to anyone and you don't need to. You don't even try to be a holy person. By now I realise that whatever has happened to me, is all God's work, and I have been the lucky recipient.

As I grow old I don't spend much time admiring myself and therefore any time I have I spend admiring God who has done so much to me, and for me – and for no good reason. Fr Richard Rohr once wrote: 'God creates wild flowers in hidden valleys that no human eye will ever see – just for the joy and beauty of it.'

By now I am happy enough simply to be human. I do not worry too much about the spiritual life, because I am not sure what it is. For me everything is both spiritual and material at the same time. I have met my worst enemy and my worst enemy is me. I have faced the shadow side of my life and found out that God loves me best in and through my mistakes.

I do not have to pretend that my religion is the only one that gets people to God. God gets people. To quote Richard Rohr again: 'I am who I am in the eyes of God, nothing more and nothing less.' I am grateful to Richard Rohr, whose work clears paths for me.

'The day will come when, after harnessing space, the winds, the tides, and gravitation, we shall harness for God the energies of love. And on that day, for the second time in the history of the world, we shall have discovered fire.' (Pierre Teilhard de Chardin)

Ronald Rolheiser is an influential American priest who writes extensively on matters of spirituality. In 2011 he was diagnosed with cancer. He has made a good recovery, and here are some of his thoughts on the experience which I found personally helpful:

'While undergoing cancer treatments I learned something. When I first started the treatments I began marking a calendar – day one, day two, day three – consciously putting my life on hold, putting myself into a posture of waiting, marking away the days until, in my fantasy, the treatments ended and I could live life again. But, strangely, as the days unfolded, to my own surprise, I found that I was living through one of the richer and happier periods in my life. I was finding a rich enjoyment in friendships, colleagues, work, and (on days when I could actually taste them) food and drink. The six months within which I was undergoing cancer treatment, turned out to be, to my own surprise, six happy and deeply meaningful months.

'As John Shea puts it: Life includes suffering. When you are spending all your energies to only rejoice in that part of life that does not include suffering, you will not enter into life because you will be dominated by fear and exclusion and not faith. Cancer taught me this lesson and, for that and your prayers, I am most grateful.'

When I was young Christmas was my favourite time of year. As I grow older I still think Christmas is a lovely season but I get more comfort from Easter.

The American orator Clarence W. Hall summed up my feelings perfectly when he preached: 'If Easter says anything to us today it is this: "You can put Truth in a grave but it won't stay there. You can nail it to a cross and shut it in a tomb but it will rise."'

Easter then is not a time for dusty old dogmas or arguments but is an opportunity for all of us to fan the ashes of hope, to banish doubts and to rejoice in living life to the full. The saying 'the glory of God is a human being fully alive' is attributed to the church father, Irenaeus. What he actually said is: 'The glory of God is the living human being.' Either way, the sense of our place in the mystery of God is a cause for joy.

Successful people get to work on their plans as quickly as possible; they know how to keep going when times are tough. They are committed people and commitment means doing what you said you would do long after the mood in which you said you would do it has passed. They do the right thing over and over again because good habits get good results.

I used to think the motto 'if it isn't broke, don't fix it' was sound advice. Not anymore. Of course there is a time to enjoy achievements. But if we bask in success the world will soon pass us by. The time to kick on to better things is when things are going well. *Be the best you can be* is a more fitting motto for today's world.

By now I'm convinced that when you want something you have never had, you have to try something you have never done before.

Accept the present moment as if you had chosen it for yourself. There is no better description of this new, helpful way of life presently sweeping the world called 'mindfulness'. We can take the opportunity to step out of the rat race and savour the present moment. It's what major religions have always done. 'Be still and know that I am God,' advises the psalmist.

Mindfulness is a new way of describing a very old practice, namely to be really conscious of life as it happens.

When I live for now I fret less about the future. And the journey is easier when I don't carry the past. I appreciate the value of this moment before it becomes a mere memory.

Mindfulness helps me to cherish the moment. It does not matter whether it is the best of moments or the worst of moments – it is the *only* moment I have got.

There comes a time when it is fitting to put a shape on the lessons life has taught us. Samuel Johnson, the eighteenth-century English critic, said it was by studying the little things 'that we attain the great art, of having as little misery, and as much happiness, as possible'.

One of the books I go back to constantly is Viktor Frankl's *Man's Search For Meaning,* where he writes about the three years he was imprisoned at Auschwitz and Dachau. There, despite all the brutality, he learned about love and the human spirit. In the concentration camps he remembers prisoners who, though close to death from hunger themselves, each day comforted others, and gave away their own meagre rations to strangers in greater need.

Admittedly, they were few in number, but still offered proof that you can take away everything from a person, but you cannot steal their innate goodness, nor their freedom to do what is decent.

We cannot predict what life has in store. But remember hard work is always rewarded and the ultimate failure is not to fail having tried, it is to squander our God-given talents.

It took me a long time to realise that remorse is harder to live with than failure is. So take your courage in your hands, give it a go, and have no regrets.

If you're feeling stressed, just remember these consoling words from St Matthew's Gospel: 'Come to me all who are overburdened and I will give you rest.' That is truly reassurance for when we feel we cannot cope.

A good listener is a rarity. It takes courage to speak up but it takes even more courage to listen well. So it is a wise counsellor who enables others to speak freely and honestly. An ancient Greek philosopher, Diogenes, says that we are given two ears and only one tongue, so that we might listen more and talk less!

To listen well means being able to hear the pain of what is *not* said; to recognise the hurt expressed in both words *and* silences. Listen to understand rather than to judge. Then it is possible to become aware of not only words, but the feelings that cannot be put into words.

Wisdom tells me that without silence, words lose their meaning. Without listening I may miss the opportunity to heal. When you rearrange the letters in SILENT you get the word LISTEN.

I get so involved trying to do good that I convince myself the world would grind to a halt if I stopped. That's complete nonsense and, worse still, it is arrogant. The truth is if I died today the world wouldn't miss a beat.

It is not that I or you do not matter – we do. It is just that our jobs, our families, our friends need us when we are around but learn to get on just as well when we are not here.

I should be sensible enough to know when I need a break – a time when I neither think of problems nor search for solutions. To just be …

The Daffodil Principle

In 1958 Gene Bauer started planting daffodils in the garden behind her house in the San Bernardino Mountains in California. She planted more bulbs every year and now there are more than one million bulbs on five acres of hillside – there are three to ten flowers per bulb. Even though it was a private garden, Gene and her husband, who helped with laying pathways and seating areas, opened their garden to the public, free of charge, when the flowers were in bloom.

A wildfire in the mountains destroyed their home in 1997 and scarred the mountainside as it burned its way through. But the daffodils bloomed as usual the following spring – a symbol of hope and joy.

The persistence of this one person doing a small thing, but doing it consistently and well over forty-six years, produced a masterpiece.

I firmly believe in the absolute importance of the good, consistent little choices we make every day, often without even being aware of them. That's what gives us character – the small, unseen, unspectacular choices to do the right thing, especially when nobody knows about them.

Jesus taught his followers: 'Whoever can be trusted in little things can also be trusted in great things …' (Lk 16:10).

Honesty, loyalty, courage, as well as kindness, patience, goodness and compassion are the bulbs I can go on planting one at a time, transforming the barren landscapes of my life. In the end, character is what counts because your character is what you really are, while your reputation is merely what other people think you are.

We all know the five stages of grief outlined by the late Dr Elisabeth Kübler-Ross. To know these five stages is helpful but is not a solution. The five stages are – denial, anger, bargaining, depression and acceptance. Kübler-Ross herself knew that they were a help in learning to live with loss. They are tools to help us identify what we may be feeling. They are not stops on some timeline of grief. So be aware of them but don't offer them as a cure.

In his book, *Out of Solitude*, Henri Nouwen says: 'When we honestly ask ourselves which person in our lives means the most to us, we often find that it is those who, instead of giving advice, solutions, or cures, have chosen rather to share our pain and touch our wounds with a warm and tender hand. The friend who can be silent with us in a moment of despair or confusion, who can stay with us in an hour of grief and bereavement, who can tolerate not knowing, not curing, not healing and face with us the reality of our powerlessness, that is a friend who cares.'

We need to learn that the first part of grief is loss, but eventually we recognise that the second part is the remaking of a life. We cannot hope to regain the life we had because that is gone. But a new life awaits us. It may be better or it may be worse but it is not the same life. It's hard to understand, but once we realise that, it's the beginning of healing.

Albert Einstein, the father of modern physics, was so fed up with the unfairness of the system that he gave up his career for a time as soon as he got his degrees. Later in life, when he was world famous, he reflected: 'I achieve results, not because I'm so smart, but because I stay with problems longer.'

It's true that we can never accurately predict what the results of hard work will be; what we do know is that if we do nothing there will be no results.

Society is based on respect for the individuals who make it up. Justice is at the heart of the common good and is the basis on which authority earns the right to be respected. The individual person's dignity is what society should be about. Society should be ordered in such a way that it advances the dignity and talents of each individual. Respect for the human person inevitably means respect for the rights that accrue from that dignity. These rights are more important than the rights of society are. They come before the rights of society.

Respect for the human person gives moral legitimacy to authority. If society is not based on respect, authority has to resort to force to get its way. Respect and dialogue are essential for a society to thrive in a creative way. A well-ordered society must first of all care for its most disadvantaged, vulnerable members. Every person has some gifts but not all are equally talented. The more talented must put their gifts at the disposal of the less well off, yet the less talented also have much to offer.

It is basic justice that workers are paid a wage which allows them to live fully human lives and to fulfil their family obligations in a dignified manner. I believe that work is there for the worker rather than the worker being there for the work. Work should be judged by the dignity it gives to the person who carries it out. The worker is to be valued more than capital is because the worker's labour causes production which results in capital.

Morality starts with respect for the dignity and proper treatment of our fellow human beings.

One of the most important documents that Pope Francis will ever publish is the encyclical letter *Laudato Si'*, which puts care of the environment as a central moral issue which all people, not just Christians, must face. Pope Francis makes it clear that he accepts scientific conclusions about the environment and challenges politicians and religious leaders and all people to change the way we live, so that the earth will be saved and the poor cared for.

The pope uses the encyclical, one of the most authoritative and binding forms of church teaching, to give weight to his arguments that good science contradicts those who live in denial or play down the severity of the environmental crisis facing us. He quotes liberally from documents issued by Bishops' Conferences around the world to back up his teaching and to show that the environment is not a personal hobbyhorse but rather a universal moral issue.

He states clearly: 'We know that technology based on the use of highly polluting fossil fuels – especially coal, but also oil, and, to a lesser degree gas – needs to be progressively replaced without delay. Furthermore we need to hear the cry of the earth and the cry of the poor.' He says: 'All of us are linked to creation. We are a part of nature, included in it, and thus in interaction with it.'

He highlights the challenge to live by the philosophy of 'Less is More'. There is an extreme consumerism whereby people are unable to resist buying what is advertised, whether they need that product or not.

The document calls for a change of heart and is addressed to every person on the planet to take part in a 'bold cultural revolution'. Francis uses vivid language to say that we have turned the earth into 'an immense pile of filth'. However, he is not without hope: 'God is with us, and we can strive both individually and corporately to change course. We can awaken our hearts to move towards an ecological conversion in which we see the connection between God and all beings and more readily to listen to "the cry of the earth and the poor".'

The title *Laudato Si'* comes from St Francis of Assisi's famous thirteenth-century prayer, 'The Canticle of the Creatures'. It's difficult to translate, but it means 'Be praised,' and is a prayer of thanksgiving to God for creation.

The *New York Times* once ran an editorial to mark Father's Day. The ten tips to fathers make good sense any day of the year:

1. It is impossible to raise a hang-up free child. Wanting perfect children is a hang-up in itself.

2. The way my children speak to each other is an accurate reflection of the way my wife and I speak to each other. Children are both sponges and mirrors.

3. Holding my children accountable for their own choices and decisions gives them the best shot at maturity.

4. Every criticism I give must be balanced at some point by a sign of acceptance and praise.

5. My children need my time, a lot of it – reading a story, fixing a broken toy or playing games are all of more value than working a sixty-hour week for things they do not really need.

6. There can never be too much laughter or music in a home.

7. Touching is more important than talking.

8. The child who drives me crazy making himself unlovable, is the child who needs my love the most.

9. If a child is without grandparents, serious consideration should be given to adopting some. Life's bumpy road with mum and dad calls for a good pair of shock absorbers.

10. I must try not to be afraid or ashamed to ask for help when my own resources as a father fail me.

According to a recent survey the world's religious leaders have a problem – the public are interested in you, but are not interested in what you say or teach.

It seems that many religious leaders are personally well known today but fewer people take any notice of what they have to say. The most effective leaders are those whose lives correspond with what they teach and preach. The public look at how they live and how they put their words into practice. They are prepared to listen only to those who practise what they preach. Integrity is the key word.

I regularly look out for different versions of familiar Bible passages. Fresh translations bring a fresh approach.

When Jesus saw his ministry drawing huge crowds, he climbed a hillside. Those who were apprenticed to him, the committed, climbed with him. Arriving at a quiet place, he sat down and taught his climbing companions. This is what he said:

'You're blessed when you're at the end of your tether. With less of you there is more of God and his rule.

'You're blessed when you feel you've lost what is most dear to you. Only then can you be embraced by the One most dear to you.

'You're blessed when you're content with just who you are – no more, no less. That's the moment you find yourselves proud owners of everything that can't be bought.

'You're blessed when you've worked up a good appetite for God. He's food and drink in the best meal you'll ever eat.

'You're blessed when you care. At the moment of being "careful", you find yourselves cared for.

'You're blessed when you get your inside world – your mind and heart – put right. Then you can see God in the outside world.

'You're blessed when you can show people how to co-operate instead of compete or fight. That's when you discover who you really are, and your place in God's family.

'You're blessed when your commitment to God provokes persecution. The persecution drives you even deeper into God's kingdom.'

(From *The Message Bible*'s version of The Beatitudes, Mt 5:1–12)

I was delighted to read a piece of advice which Pope Francis gave nineteen newly ordained priests earlier this year. He told them that all of us, priests and people alike, share in the mission of the church; it's not just reserved for clerics.

To highlight this point he told them how important it is that their preaching should be down to earth and relevant to people's lives. 'Dispense to all the Word of God,' he said, 'that which you yourselves have received with joy. Read and think about the Word of the Lord so that you will believe what you read. If you believe it then you will teach what you have learned in faith, and most importantly, you will live yourself what you have taught.'

Fr Thomas Reese, a well-known Jesuit writer, wrote: 'I promised myself that I would never say anything from the pulpit that I did not believe or that I did not at least want to believe. I would not pretend to be more than I am.'

Preaching demands authenticity. The congregation knows when words do not come from the heart. 'This does not mean the priest is coming down from the mountain with inspiration from God. Rather, it often means that the priest is struggling up the mountain with the People of God.'

I couldn't have put it better myself!

George Bernard Shaw is credited with saying: 'A life spent making mistakes is not only more honourable, but more useful, than a life spent doing nothing.' Pope Francis agrees with Mr Shaw. For the first time in living memory we have a pope who freely and openly admits he can be wrong, make mistakes, and is willing to do something about it.

There is an interesting trend in many of the statements made by the current pope. Following the death of John XXIII, the papacy became suffocated by pride. The pope and those who spoke on his behalf, were 'always right'. They spoke on God's behalf, they claimed, and so they could never admit they were wrong; they could never apologise. As a result, they lost credibility, particularly in countries where the population has had the opportunity for, and access to, education. Common sense tells us that as human beings we all make mistakes. To claim infallibility for every pronouncement of the pope lacks integrity.

Worse still, in more recent years the entire Vatican organisation was at pains to pretend that every statement made by the pope could be infallible; that when the pope spoke he was always teaching. Therefore it became part of this mysterious concept called the magisterium. It meant that even the most indefensible statement could not be challenged, discussed or questioned.

This made the Catholic Church appear idiotic.

Pope Francis, in his own subtle way, makes it quite clear that he is willing to be challenged on the many opinions he expresses about world events, both religious and secular. He's at pains to assure us that he believes what he says but recognises he could be wrong. He's prepared to listen, to change his opinions, to admit his mistakes and to argue his point.

A person has to be brave enough to admit mistakes, quick enough to learn from them, and big enough to correct them. My mistakes are always forgivable *only* after I have the courage to admit them. As the great coach John Wooden said: 'If you are not making mistakes, then you are not doing anything.' It's common sense to know it's possible to do things better. We learn by having an open mind to fair criticism and by being willing to change course so that we can be revitalised in a healthy way. This is a path that the church leadership needs to choose to remain on if it is to carry out its main function of bringing the good news to all.

Care of our world is not just the moral duty of Christians and other responsible people but is part and parcel of the rich and full life given to us by God. The pope's encyclical *Laudato Si'* is a clear call for all people to live responsibly on this earth.

In one of his most insightful quotes, the pope pleads: 'There are symptoms of sickness evident in the soil and in the water, that the earth herself, burdened and laid waste, is among the most abandoned, maltreated of our poor ... Therefore sister earth now cries to us because of the harm we have inflicted on her by our irresponsible use and abuse of the goods with which God has endowed her.'

Pope Francis, like St Francis before him, encourages us to examine our lifestyle and to make the necessary changes.

I was fascinated with the challenge broadcaster Adrian Chiles set himself during Lent. He decided to go to church every day during Lent and never the same church twice. Why did he do it? 'I'm a Catholic, so it would be Mass every day for more than a month. It felt like it would be a real struggle – a penance. It turned out to be anything but. It was a rich and enriching experience – spiritually obviously, but I was also enraptured by the churches themselves, the communities they serve, and the people with whom I shared all those Masses,' Chiles admitted.

He made it more difficult for himself by promising to go to a different church every day. He reckons at the end of Lent he had been with forty-six different priests, in forty-six different churches, on forty-six days.

Chiles had some wry comments to make about the priests he met on his forty-six-day journey: 'It was all a mixed bag, as were the priests. A third of them I found to be great, with a handful quite life-challengingly brilliant. The other third were a sort of okay. The rest were pretty hopeless, not least because I often couldn't actually hear what they were saying. And a handful were grumpy to the point of malevolence.

'Spiritually, if I am to really take an active role at Mass I need a good priest to help me. And by good I mean first and foremost that they should look pleased to be there and pleased that we are there. Often they speak of great "joy" while looking as bored as swimming pool attendants.

'My favourite homily ever came from my first priest (I'm a convert), a Fr Tastard, a man with an unforgettable name in the happy habit of delivering pretty unforgettable homilies. At one weekly Mass he simply said: "How is it that we are always so keen for others to change, when we are so reluctant to change ourselves?"'

As I look at life I have now come to believe in the God of 'somehow'. Life happens somehow. We get through it somehow. We overcome the crosses and the crises somehow. God accompanies the sick through terrible times somehow and people survive somehow. God is journeying with the bereaved as he was on the road to Emmaus and the grieving people often do not know that God is silently walking alongside them. But somehow they know strength is coming to them. We get though life somehow. We get over anger and disappointment and denial somehow.

I have worked all my life as a priest and often wonder, like teachers and parents do, why it is that people do not seem to care for the things that are so important, like prayer, faith, morals, belief in God and a love of the Mass. So many do not acknowledge God or even pray. But still God loves them somehow and often gets through to them in the most mysterious ways. It is sad that sometimes families turn up for Communion and Confirmation and then disappear. But we have to know that the seed of Communion and Confirmation and good example, and happy times, is planted in their lives and somehow will grow in its own good time.

Clodagh Cogley, one of the students who was severely injured in the Berkeley balcony collapse in 2015, posted a message online shortly before she was to leave hospital and move to a rehabilitation centre in San Francisco. It read:

'Hey friends, just an update to let you know how I'm getting on … The fall from the balcony left me with two collapsed lungs, a broken shoulder, a broken knee, five broken ribs and a broken spinal cord … meaning the chances of me using my legs again are pretty bleak. … Who knows maybe my legs have been holding me back all these years and I'll realise my talent for wheelchair basketball!

'The thing I'm taking from this tragedy is that life is short and I intend to honour those who died by living the happiest and most fulfilling life possible. Enjoy a good dance and the feeling of grass beneath your feet like it's the last time because, in this crazy world, you never know when it might be.'

St Paul in his second letter to the Corinthians tells us that he was given 'a thorn in the flesh' to keep him grounded (2 Cor 12:7–10). According to scripture scholars, this 'thorn' was not a physical or emotional disturbance, but most likely hostility directed at him from others within his own Christian communities. He found this difficult and prayed that 'it would leave me'. But the answer to his prayer was not to remove the thorn, rather it was to understand that God's grace is sufficient for him. Counteracting the hostility was not to set himself up against it, boasting about his achievements or his commitments to his faith and evangelising work. He had to face it in his weakness, in his understanding that through this weakness Christ's power is worked through him.

Do we recognise the Spirit in those we resent, in those who challenge our conceptions of faith and religion?

The term 'vocation' has been long associated with religious vocation. The word vocation comes from the Latin word *vocare*, meaning 'to call'. But we are *all* called by God, not just the tiny proportion of the population who believe they have a religious calling. What are we called for? That is our challenge in life, to understand what we are being asked to do.

John Henry Newman experienced God's call in his life. It was not just one calling, but several. The challenge was to know when a change of direction was part of that call. Many of us like to get to a comfortable place in our lives where we do not feel challenged, where we believe we have 'figured it out', whatever 'it' is. John Henry Newman was anything but comfortable. When he left the Anglican communion to convert to Catholicism, he lost many friends. When he put his formidable intellect at the service of the Catholic Church, he found himself 'out in the cold' and treated with suspicion by the very church he gave up everything for. His biggest mistake was to suggest the experience of the laity had something to offer the church leadership in matters of doctrine. Yet, his faith sustained him. He had a deep trust in God:

'God has created me to do Him some definite service. He has committed some work to me which He has not committed to another. I have my mission. I may never know it in this life, but I shall be told it in the next. I am a link in a chain, a bond of connection between persons. He has not created me for naught. I shall do good; I shall do His work. I shall be an angel of peace, a preacher of truth in my own place, while not intending it if I do but keep His commandments. Therefore, I will trust him, whatever I am, I can never be thrown away. If I am in sickness, my sickness may serve Him, in perplexity, my perplexity may serve Him. If I am in sorrow, my sorrow may serve Him. He does nothing in vain. He knows what He is about. He may take away my friends. He may throw me among strangers. He may make me feel desolate, make my spirits sink, hide my future from me. Still, He knows what He is about.'

'"Woe to the shepherds who destroy and scatter the sheep of my pasture!" says the Lord. Therefore thus says the Lord, the God of Israel, concerning the shepherds who shepherd my people: "It is you who have scattered my flock, and have driven them away, and you have not attended to them. So I will attend to you for your evil doings," says the Lord.'

That passage of scripture is from the prophet Jeremiah. Jeremiah was an interesting man. He was called by God to challenge the people and leaders of his time for their false worship and social injustice. He did not want the job and cursed, vehemently, the day that he was born. This is hardly surprising as his life was in danger because of the things he was saying. Other prophets told the king what he wanted to hear. Jeremiah told him what he needed to hear. His life was so difficult; he tried to ignore his prophetic calling but, as he says in his prayer, even if he resolved not to speak, he could not help himself, his vocation was like a 'burning fire' in him.

Jeremiah was speaking of the kings of Judah in the passage above, but his cry can be applied to the religious leaders of our times. To what extent are leaders preaching the message of peace, social justice, care for all, especially in the three Abrahamic faiths: Judaism, Christianity and Islam – the faiths 'of the Book' as they are often called? What kind of witnesses are we to the God of love who speaks so passionately about justice rather than power and control?

We can do without the divisive fanaticism which religion sometimes brings. Yet, I also hold that a genuine belief in the spiritual helps to shape society in a positive way. People of faith are encouraged to be less selfish; we use our gifts for the benefit of our neighbours; we foster respect for ourselves and others. In my experience those whose lives are guided by faith tend to be less greedy and are more grateful for what they have.

I love the writings of a renowned expert in prayer, Anthony Bloom, who was leader of the Russian Orthodox Church in Britain and Ireland. I was surprised to learn that towards the end of his life he admitted much of his prayer was based on a flawed belief – namely that if he stopped praying the world would collapse. A wise friend told him he should depend more on God's mercy and less on his own efforts. As an experiment, the friend suggested he should actually stop praying for a month. Instead, he should sit quietly and simply say: 'May the prayers of those who love me, save me.' Then he should allow images of those friends whom he believed loved him, to float around in his imagination – acknowledge each of them and thank God for their love.

Anthony did as he was told and very soon realised that whether he prayed or not, God loved him anyway. Afterwards prayer became easy because all his prayers were 'thank yous'.

I believe that faith, prayer and gratitude might not change the *facts* of life, but they do have the power to make my life more manageable and more peaceful.

Many lives have been traumatised, brutalised and ruined by sexual abuse. Each experience of abuse took its toll on countless lives, relationships, futures. An immeasurable number of hearts and lives have been broken. We recognise these broken hearts and shattered lives, the human beings behind the statistics: the direct victims, their families, their friends and colleagues; the perpetrators, their families, their friends and colleagues; you and me and all who hold the pain of abuse or its effects in their hearts.

The road to healing is a long one. It has many twists and turns and there may be setbacks. Listen to one person who shares their hurt: 'I hated myself to the point where I simply wanted to die. I did not know how to nurture or take care of myself.

'I was afraid to succeed because I felt I was not worthy.

'But since I have faced up to my abuse I have come to realise I am a very courageous, worthwhile person. I am learning to be good to my poor body which has become so broken. I thank God for giving me the help of excellent people – therapist, doctor, family and a few good friends. I thank God for giving me the strength to continue the journey of counselling even though at times it was sheer hell. It is as if a fog has lifted from my eyes.

'I give thanks for good things in my life, like my children and my long suffering partner. I now know that the abuse will never have the power to take my life away again.

'I am still not able to forgive the person who abused me. Maybe someday it will come.'

We especially remember those who continue to struggle with a personal experience of abuse. We remember too those families who have suffered so much as they witnessed the trauma experienced by loved ones. We pray for those in caring groups who listen to and support survivors as they share their painful stories and we pray for society that it will support recovery and healing at every level.

Help each one of us to recognise the harm that has been done, but never forget the goodness that still remains within each of us.

I have been thinking a lot about prejudice, violence, and the need for forgiveness. I am convinced we will never have true peace here – or anywhere – until we learn to deal with hurt in a real way. It means learning to live with forgiveness, and to leave the *past* behind so that we can have a peaceful *future*. If we deliberately hold on to the past, we shouldn't be surprised if we become prisoners of it.

To move on, we need to be able to see good, even in our enemies. At times like this, I always go back to Nelson Mandela's autobiography, *Long Walk to Freedom*. In one story, he describes the callous regime on Robben Island, which was cruel and inhuman for the prisoners. It was so bad that a mediator arrived to help solve the problem. Mandela bravely explained at the open meeting who was responsible for the cruelty.

The next day the captain in charge, the man named by Mandela, called the prisoners together and told them he was leaving the island. He went on to wish each of the prisoners, including Nelson Mandela, every success and happiness for the future. This shocked Mandela and he was forced to admit that 'all men, even brutal men, have a core of decency.' Ever after, Mandela judged everyone, especially his enemies, more kindly. That eased his bitter resentment which had, up to then, destroyed his inner peace.

It's a good lesson for all of us and one which actually permeates the Bible. Perhaps the most helpful insight of all comes from St Paul's letter to the Romans (13:8–10). There we are told: 'Love is the one thing that cannot hurt your neighbour.' *There's* a great thought to hold on to today. It's hard to put into practice. But then look at the pictures of hate on your television and see how painful the alternative is.

In the Jesuit House in Leeson Street, Dublin, a painting hung on the wall above the mantelpiece in the dining room, depicting the arrest of Jesus in Gethsemane. When they were redecorating the house somebody with a keen eye suggested that it should be valued. After many experts were consulted, it turned out the painting was the work of the great Italian artist, Caravaggio. *The Taking of Christ* was restored and it now hangs in the National Gallery of Ireland and is one of the gallery's greatest treasures.

For all those years that it hung in the dining room it was always a treasure, but nobody knew it. It went unrecognised. It hung on the wall waiting to be discovered. Now everyone wonders how such a work of art was ignored for so long.

There's a helpful passage in St Paul's Letter to the Ephesians which says: 'We are God's work of art created in Christ to live the good life' (Eph 2–10).

I don't know about you but I don't normally think of myself as a work of art. If I am, no one else has noticed. But perhaps, like the painting on the wall, somebody will someday.

It is encouraging that God sees each of us as a work of art. He said through the prophet Isaiah: 'You are precious in my sight and I love you.'

There are people whom I regard as works of art and I treasure them for it. But I still think of myself as being, at best, cobbled together. St Paul says that's okay too: 'You are a work of art, not for anything you have done but simply because God made us in God's own image.' I am a genuine work of art whether I know it or not.

Go to a mirror, turn on the light, look at yourself, wink and say: 'You really are a beautiful work of art.' If you do it often enough you might one day believe it.

Years ago, Woody Allen appeared on television for a rare personal interview. He spoke about the many and complicated romantic relationships he was involved in. He even talked about the dating experiences he had whilst at college. Woody recalled a wonderful relationship which lasted for seven years. They were even talking about marriage, he volunteered. So naturally, he was asked why they parted. In a characteristically witty response Woody said the relationship went sour because of what he called serious religious differences: 'I was an agnostic and she was an atheist.' Typical Woody Allen!

To some he is the most unfunny man on earth. For others, and I admit I am one of these, he is a genius who forces us to laugh ourselves into the truth. Truth and love are two of the most powerful forces on earth. When they come together they're hard to ignore. Add humour and they are impossible to resist.

These days most of us are too busy to think about truth or to reflect on life at all. The great paradox of our time is that we are busy and bored at the same time. Our lives are filled like over-packed suitcases bursting at the seams. No matter how much we *do*, there is *always* something left to do. Worse still, we are not sure whether it would make any difference if we did nothing at all. Our lives are at the same time full and unfulfilled.

That is enough to drive anyone mad unless we are humble enough to recognise the need for healthy relationships and true friends who will challenge us, affirm us and steer us to a sense of self-worth.

I believe that good friends are a really precious gift. There is something sacred about a friend who listens and gently coaxes me to think, reflect, change and grow. Someone who stays with me in times of despair and confusion; who walks with me in grief and sadness; who can tolerate not knowing everything about me; who doesn't have to cure me; who faces me with the reality of my life, both good and bad – people like that are among the greatest gifts God gives us. This morning I'm grateful that God has blessed me with a few of those precious, treasured friends and I hope you have some in your life too.

A tiny acorn has the potential to become not just a mighty oak tree, but a thousand oak trees. We humans have within us the seeds of unlimited potential. And yet that limitless potential can be stifled by one little emotion – fear. Fear of failure can kill our emotions stone dead.

That's why courage is such an important gift to have. Courage is not the absence of fear, which can, in fact, be foolishness. Courage helps us to act in spite of our genuine fears.

The psychotherapist Jim Colfer says that FEAR can be challenged, by thinking of the word differently: F-E-A-R – Face Everything And Recover.

I believe love is the best antidote to fear. I once heard a widowed mother of eight children explain love marvellously. She was asked if she loved all her children equally. She replied that she loved them all but *not* equally: 'I loved the one the most who felt a failure until he began to feel good about himself; I loved the one the most who was weak until she felt strong; I loved the one the most who was hurt until he was healed; I loved the one the most who was lost until she was found.'

There is a prayer which all Christians say regularly and which disturbs me greatly when I think about it. It is the Lord's Prayer. The part which disturbs me most is: 'Forgive us our trespasses (our sins) *as* we forgive those who trespass against us.' That means God's forgiveness of me depends on the way I forgive others.

Forgiveness is necessary for healthy living but is never easy. There is no cheap way to forgive. There is no quick fix. It comes slowly and has to be constantly renewed. We cannot forgive on our own. We need help, especially God's help, to do it.

People often say, 'forgive and forget'. I don't agree. Forgiveness is not the same as forgetting. Part of the process is to let go of festering hurts but that is not the same as forgetting. Forgiveness requires a change of heart. Neither is forgiveness mere indifference. We have to make sure that the hurt or the evil will not be repeated and we have to realise that those who hurt us are not all bad. Keep things in perspective.

When I forgive someone I am also agreeing to give *myself* a fresh start. I also have to allow the other person a chance to start afresh too. It is not a cold war. Wrong was done, but the person has more to offer. Look for goodness and affirm it.

Perhaps this next point is the most difficult to put into practice. It means that we wish the person who hurt us well in life. Let God be their judge. I hand them over to God's care knowing that I will need God's mercy myself. That is the only way we can genuinely and sincerely wish them well.

As with all feelings that is the theory. Putting it into practice is not easy – unless of course, we think of what refusing to forgive does to us.

We celebrate the Harvest Thanksgiving in our church at the Graan in Enniskillen every year. In one of the prayers we thank God for 'heaven all around us'. This got me thinking about heaven – something I rarely do.

The American preacher Bishop Fulton Sheen, a famous TV preacher in the 1960s, used to tell this story against himself.

He was due to preach in Philadelphia, which is an unusual American city in that it is not laid out in blocks. Bishop Sheen was staying in a hotel and wanted to walk to the town hall, which was just a half a mile away. However, he got lost and half an hour later he ended up back at the hotel entrance.

There were two boys playing on the street. He had to swallow his pride and ask them to direct him to the town hall. 'What do you want to go there for?' one of the kids asked. 'I am giving a talk,' he replied. 'What are you talking about?' 'I'm giving a talk on how to get to heaven.' And then he added: 'Would you like to come along to listen?' To which the one of the boys replied: 'How to get to heaven? Not likely sir. You can't even get to the town hall.' The lad had a point. We preachers tell people how to get to heaven but run the risk of getting lost ourselves.

But heaven is *always* nearby if we have the vision to see it. The poet Elizabeth Barrett Browning, has a beautiful piece which highlights this. She says:

> … Earth's crammed with heaven,
> And every common bush afire with God;
> But only he who sees, takes off his shoes,
> The rest sit round it and pluck blackberries.

It's a beautiful image: earth is crammed with heaven. But only genuine searchers recognise it as holy ground and take off their shoes. The rest get lost in life's rush.

The late Irish novelist and journalist, Maeve Binchy, humorously recalled a conversation with her mother who was effortlessly passing on words of wisdom to her. 'Always remember', she told Maeve, 'that *how are you*, is a greeting, not a question.'

It reminded me of a kindly old monk who lived in the community over twenty years ago. He was always capable of passing on a truth wrapped in a cynical jibe. One morning when he was old and close to death, I sat beside him as he rearranged a small portion of porridge around his plate. I asked, 'How are you this morning?' 'Brian,' he said, with a delightful, impish grin, 'over the years I've learned that the definition of a bore is someone who, when you ask them how they are, tell you.'

It is true. 'How are you' can often be the opening a person needs to begin an elaborate catalogue of miseries – 'my eyes are failing,' 'my knees are aching,' 'I'm crippled with arthritis.' And, if you are a man with a cold, 'I'm dying with the flu.'

However, genuine concern for others is one of the best gifts we can give to our friends in these tough, impersonal times. As a priest, I've discovered that *how* I listen is far more helpful than words of advice I might manage to pass on. I listen with my eyes and with my body language, as much as with my ears. People do not hear compassion – they feel it, experience it.

The American writer Rachel Naomi Remen tells a powerful story about a brilliant doctor she knew, who had to work hard on his bedside manner, with some success. One day a grateful patient presented him with an ornate stethoscope which had his name engraved on it. He asked what prompted such an unusual present. 'Because *you* listen to hearts,' she told him.

That is the secret isn't it? 'How are you' can be a meaningless greeting. Or it can be an invitation for a real heart-to-heart healing encounter.

A group of ten-year-olds in a geography class were asked to name what they considered to be the Seven Wonders of the World. The Taj Mahal, the Grand Canyon, Victoria Falls, and the Great Wall of China were in every list. One girl was having difficulty putting anything on paper. When the teacher asked why she was struggling, she admitted there were so many wonders of the world she couldn't make up her mind.

'Well, tell us what you have and we'll help you,' the teacher suggested. Shyly she stood up and read: 'The seven wonders of the world are,' and she whispered her list, 'to touch, to taste, to see, to hear …' She looked up and hesitated for a moment before continuing, 'to run, to laugh, to love.' That little girl truly did understand the important things in life and where happiness lies.

Robert Louis Stevenson (who lived in the latter half of the nineteenth century) made a list of the attitudes which made him happy in life. Here are a few of them:

1. Make up your mind to be happy.
2. Learn to find pleasures in simple things.
3. Don't take yourself too seriously.
4. You can't please everybody, so don't let criticism cripple you.
5. Be yourself and do the things you enjoy doing.
6. Do what you can for those less fortunate than yourself.
7. Keep busy at something. A busy person never has time to be unhappy.

Times are tough and many people find it hard to make ends meet. One of the many letters I received came from a mother telling me about her married daughter who had a major accident which left her confined to a wheelchair. She and her small children were rehoused to an upstairs flat, which was impossible for her. She even found rats in the bedroom!

At the end of the letter the mother added: 'When you are poor with no money, the future's always in another place.' And who could argue with that?

Many of us though, willingly condemn ourselves to the same hopeless future when we refuse to change or search for new ways of living. Hell has been described as an eternity locked into the present with no possibility of change. Yet, mostly, life *has* possibilities.

'Live each day as if it were your last and one day you'll be right,' is good advice. Living for today is not easy in the modern world. Did you ever stop to think what you would do if you were told the end of your life was near? It happens to people every day. I do not know how I would react if I was told that news.

Cardinal Newman, who has been beatified by the Catholic Church, once said: 'To grow is to change, and to be perfect is to change often.' He also said: 'To be holy is not so much *doing* this or *not* doing that … but is a state of mind of living habitually in the light of a better world.'

No matter how tough life is, it will not last forever – there is always hope.

As an old bachelor looking on, I'm always delighted when a couple start their marriage so obviously in love and I hope their love will grow and grow every day of their lives.

The late Frank Muir worked for many years in the BBC. Frank was married for thirty-nine years to a girl whom he met halfway between the beans and the toast in the BBC canteen. He recalled that he fell in love with her at first sight and remained in love with her to the day he died.

He mused as to how this show business marriage lasted so long. And surprisingly, he said that although he and his wife were from different religions they always prayed together each night. At the end of the prayers he told his wife he loved her and she affirmed her love for him too.

In his typical offbeat way, Frank concluded that when the tabloids asked him, as they frequently did, how often did he tell his wife he loved her, he could quite truthfully answer: 'At least 14,000 times.'

Whether in or out of relationships, we all need somebody to love us. And it is even better when they tell us.

Looking at couples, as I have, for nearly fifty years in ministry now, there are just a few golden rules which I think help to make a marriage work. The first is this. Even a stopped clock is right twice a day. So, when people have stopped growing, they can still have something to offer.

A good partnership is not so much about marrying the right person as *being* the right person. A good principle to recognise is that contentment is not getting what we *want*, but being satisfied with what we *have*. Even a reluctant bachelor like me recognises that as the secret of a happy marriage and indeed a happy life.

We in Ireland can sometimes be a nation of moaners! Yet there are also people of extraordinary generosity.

There is a Nigerian proverb which says: 'Give thanks for a little and you will find a lot.' I have discovered that a grateful person remains grateful under any circumstances; a complaining person will find something wrong even in heaven.

The beginning of grateful living is to realise that everything I have is given to me as a gift, starting with life itself. Before I open my eyes in the morning I can complain that I didn't sleep long enough or I can be grateful that I have eyes to open. More than forty million people in the world are blind. When I start off like that, I go through the day, moment by moment, being completely surprised about anything and everything.

If I am surprised then I will be grateful. We should try to see life as a vessel. Keep the vessel small and it will always overflow and I will always have enough. The problem with modern society is that we believe we ought to have everything we desire and so the vessel gets bigger and bigger. It can never be filled, and we are never satisfied.

So, today I intend to have a good time without wasting anything. I am going to be grateful for what I have. I am going to enjoy food without being a glutton; I am going to give away anything I do not need. The older I get the more I realise that if I have good health, good friends and a good laugh I really have all those gifts that money can't buy.

The American theologian John Shea has a simple story about trust. He tells of a man who spent his youth searching for meaning.

One day he was lucky to meet God as he journeyed on the road. He took the opportunity to seek his help: 'God, how can I find happiness?'

God said: 'I have been travelling all day – could you please get me a drink of water?'

So the man went into a village to get the drink for God. In the village he knocked on a door and a beautiful girl welcomed him. He asked her for a drink of water for God.

She said: 'Maybe you need one yourself, so come in.' He did. It was midday so they shared a beautiful lunch too. After that he couldn't leave. So he married the girl, raised a family and had a really meaningful life.

One day, after thirty years, he was out walking when a ferocious storm blew up. He cried out: 'God, please save me.' and God said: 'What about the drink of water?'

You can take many meanings out of that but one of them is that when life is going great we forget God. We call on God only when we're in trouble. But God reminds us that a relationship is a two-way street. Don't turn your back on me just because you don't need me. Keep in touch in good times and you will recognise me in bad times.

Albert Einstein once said: 'Only a life lived for others is worth living.' John Wesley, one of the founding brothers of the Methodist movement, said much the same: 'Do all the good you can, by all the means you can, in all the ways you can, at all the times you can, to all the people you can, as long as ever you can.'

An encouraging word works wonders for our morale. Yet, we rarely tell people when they do well. Worse still, cynical or ungenerous comments can be devastating.

Bob Danzig is a famous American motivational speaker and businessman. He started work as an office boy at a newspaper and ended up CEO of the Hearst Newspaper group. He credits whatever success he has to words of encouragement spoken to him at crucial times in his life by two caring individuals.

He spent his childhood moving around five different foster homes. He desperately needed to feel loved. But each time he was rejected. At the age of nine though, he was given a new social worker to help him through his difficulties. At the end of their first meeting she said to him: 'Bobby, I want you to always remember these words: You are worthwhile.' And, as he remembers it, she repeated the same words at the end of every meeting they had. In time, Bob Danzig began to believe it. It guided him through his formative years.

When he graduated from high school he got a job with a newspaper company, as a runner – the bottom rung of the ladder. He worked there for six months before his boss called him into her office. He was sure he would be sacked. Instead she said: 'I've been observing you young man and I believe you are full of promise.'

That was enough. He worked hard to fulfil the confidence she had in him. In time he rose to the very top of the newspaper industry. He now donates the money he earns from speaking engagements to foster children who, like himself, got a bad start in life. He does it because he knows that the right word at the right time changed his life.

Louis Pasteur put it well when he said: 'When I see a child

I'm inspired by two sentiments: tenderness for what he is and respect for what he may become.'

An encouraging word is one way to nurture that potential. May somebody be kind enough to help you with an encouraging word today and may you be wise enough to do the same.

My favorite prayer, which I still say every day of my life, was written by Thomas Merton, who was born just over one hundred years ago:

> My Lord God, I have no idea where I am going. I do not see the road ahead of me. I cannot know for certain where it will end. Nor do I really know my own self, and the fact that I think I am following your will does not necessarily mean that I am actually doing so. But I believe that the desire to please you does in fact please you. And I hope I have that desire in everything that I do. I hope that I will never do anything apart from that desire. And I know that if I do this, you will lead me by the right road even though I may know nothing about it. Therefore I will trust you always. Even though I may seem to be lost and in the shadow of death I will fear no evil, for you are ever with me and you will never leave me to face my peril alone.